NEW PREACHING
FROM THE
OLD TESTAMENT

NEW PREACHING FROM THE OLD TESTAMENT

D. W. Cleverley Ford

MOWBRAYS
LONDON & OXFORD

*Printed in Great Britain
at the Alden Press, Oxford*

ISBN 0 264 66096 X

*First published 1976
by A. R. Mowbray & Co Ltd
The Alden Press, Osney Mead
Oxford OX2 OEG*

CONTENTS

ACKNOWLEDGEMENTS

As with a number of my previous books, this one has been written at the invitation of Richard Mulkern, a Director of the Publishing Department of A.R. Mowbray & Co., Ltd., to whom I am indebted not only for the title, but for valuable criticisms and suggestions. The Editor of the *Expository Times* has kindly granted permission for the publication here of the sermon called 'An Old Testament Beatitude', which has already appeared in that journal. I am grateful again to Mrs J. Hodgson for preparing my manuscript for the publishers and to my wife for correcting the proofs.

Lambeth Palace 1975   *D. W. Cleverley Ford*

INTRODUCTION

'Then Samuel hewed Agag in pieces before the Lord at Gilgal. . . . ' (1 Samuel 15.33) Perhaps this verse presents in its starkest form for Christians the unacceptable face of the Old Testament. After all, Samuel was one of the most renowned of Israel's prophets; what is more, the victim was not handed over to the secular arm for capital punishment which at least was the custom with the Medieval Church. Samuel hacked at Agag himself; and as if this were not sufficient to cause us to recoil in horror, he carried out his bloodthirsty deed 'before the Lord', that is, in the recognized place of God's presence. And had Agag committed so great a crime after all? Would not modern sympathies be on his side? The Old Testament's seal set on actions such as this is one reason why Christian preachers have been embarrassed to make use of this book in preaching. But there are other grounds. It is not only the unmoral and immoral actions that baffle, but the archaisms and the sheer boredom attaching to the legal and even to some of the historical sections. All in all the Old Testament does not seem to belong to a modern Christian congregation. Not surprisingly one Cathedral reported that only one preacher throughout a whole year preached a sermon from it.

The Old Testament always has presented a problem to the Church and in general there have been three ways of attempting to solve it. First there was Marcion's way in the second century which was to eliminate it altogether. Christians who are Marcionites in this sense are not hard to find today. A second way of avoiding the difficulties was to spiritualize all that was read in the Old Testament leaving no stone unturned, to find types and analogies of Christ, moral values and homiletical advice, producing a result that was often fanciful in the extreme. A third way belongs to the late nineteenth and twentieth centuries; it consists generally in the theory of a progressive revelation in the Bible whereby the peak is reached in Christ with all that precedes it being regarded as inferior in the sense of being preparatory. Clearly on this view the Old Testament only possesses compelling interest for those studying the development of religion. It is of scant use for the preacher.

What then are we to do with the Old Testament? We should read it as a faith book, a book which records the history, customs and aspirations of a people into the patchwork of which there has filtered, sometimes purely, sometimes impurely, a practical faith in the same God as we Christians confess—but before the coming of Christ. So there is continuity between the Old Testament and the New, but also discontinuity. We shall be advised therefore not to read back the New into the Old, nor even to judge the Old in the light of the New. Promise in the Old Testament and fulfilment in the New is a justifiable way of assessing their relationship to each other but only if we are careful to let the Old Testament speak for itself, only if our aim is to discover what was the faith by which these Hebrews lived and what it has to teach us now. The Old Testament has a message of its own. It has something to proclaim. There is an Old Testament *kerygma*, and what it is can be edifying to Christians. Was not Jesus himself nourished by the Hebrew scriptures? And did he not recognize their authority? We even have in St Luke chapter four a sermon preached by him in the Nazareth synagogue, using an Old Testament text!

In the last resort, however, it is not theoretical justifications of the Old Testament that will commend its use to Christians, but expository preaching. Not until the book begins to speak to us where we are will its retention by the Church seem proper. And then the reason will lie in the discovery that we are hearing some Word of God addressed to us through its pages. In the hope that the following sermon outlines will serve this function they have been offered. They are taken from different parts of the Old Testament. They do not fall into a pattern or offer any theory of development of doctrine. They are like bits of glass scattered across the surface of the Old Testament, in the glint of which something of the glory of God has been reflected to the present writer. They have been set out (so to speak) on a bench for others in the hope that they will be encouraged to look for glories for themselves.

1 THE PROCLAMATION

Genesis 1.1 (RSV) *In the beginning God created the heavens and the earth*

Introduction

The Old Testament begins with preaching, it begins with proclamation. It proclaims God as existing before all that is, as the originator of all that is, and as the sustainer of all that is. God is the final reality, there is nothing beyond him and nothing that is not derived from him. Therefore matter is not the final reality, whatever may be the tendency of prevailing western thought; and mind is not the final reality, whatever may be traditional eastern thought. God stands supreme as regards time, all things and all ideas.

1 *God the decisive factor*

But what does this mean? What does it mean in the Old Testament? It means an introduction to a new way of looking at the world. It shows us a different kind of world from what we should have seen without it. Granted all the familiar aspects of life as we know them find their place in it. People eat, drink, sleep, marry (both for love and for convenience), lust, fornicate, fight, scheme, grow fat, die of hunger, curse God and lampoon religion. Yes, and pray, too; idolize, stay faithful and apostasize. You name it! It is all there in the Old Testament, but with this difference. God always comes into the picture. No, not merely as the scenery on the stage nor as the stage itself. God actually enters into the natural and the human drama and acts for his own purpose.

Can this divine presence in the world be proved? Does the Old Testament make the attempt? It does not. The Old Testament is a faith book, a *Glaubensbuch*, as Bonhöffer expressed it. It proclaims a faith by which those who will listen are called to live. It declares the living God to be the decisive factor in every situation.

I

2 God the Sustainer

What then does creation mean? Not that God produced a machine called the universe and then withdrew leaving it to operate independently of himself. Such was the error of the eighteenth century thinkers called the Deists. Creation is the initial and continuous activity of God on behalf of, and within, all that exists. Translated into every day language and brought down to the human level, it asserts that your world and my world exist *because God sustains them*; and if God ceased to be, both you and I, and our world, would cease to be. Not that the reverse would also be true—not that if you and I, and our world, ceased to be, God would cease to be. This would imply pantheism, that is, the belief that God and the world are identical—God is all, and all is God. On the contrary, if all ceased to be, God would still exist. This absolute supremacy of God is what the doctrine of God as creator implies.

3 God sustains freedom

So then God sustains our world. He even sustains our freedom in it. An illustration of this is given in W. E. Hocking's book called *Science and the Idea of God* (1944). Think of a motion picture being projected on to a screen. The drama proceeds as long as the light in the projector shines. The light does not make the figures in the drama perform, but it sustains their activity. If the light fails, the drama fails. So God is not responsible for everything we do, or for everything that is done in the world. This is not what creation means. It means instead that God sustains the world, including our freedom and all within it.

Perhaps we could take this idea a step further. Think of God as the sunlight and the world as a garden. What the sunlight does is to draw out the potential life in the soil, thus producing all manner of growth, variety and beauty. Where there is no sunlight there is little growth, and even less beauty and variety. But when the sun arises all is changed. There is life and colour and brilliance. Darkness means death. Light means life. What is more, it means a certain independent life, because potentiality is developed. So even aberration and the peculiar are possible, and with them both the possibility of disaster and tragedy. So God, as the creator is not the direct originator of all that takes place. That tragic loss of life in the earthquake in Turkey in 1975 cannot be laid directly at his door, nor the couple that were shot in their own home by terrorists in Belfast. God sustains the life of the world including its independence either to respond to him and live, or to fail to respond and die. These are the terms in which God as creator is to be understood, and without such an interpretation of Genesis chapter one, Genesis chapter three, the story of the fall of man in the Garden of Eden, does not make sense; but what is more important, our own world does not make sense. We believe, we should believe, that God is the Sovereign Lord of the universe, being its creator, but we also know that we are free, free even to reject him.

APPEAL

Understanding, however, is not what preaching seeks chiefly to provide. It seeks rather an act of will, looking for a response in the sphere of practical living. It prays and it hopes that those who hear of God as creator and sustainer will be sensitive to the reality of this God in their own life story, the story being made today and tomorrow and the day following. This scripture calls us to trust in a power beyond ourselves issuing in courage and producing the energy necessary for purposeful involvement in our day-to-day world. Such a faith is dynamic. It changes people and they change situations. It comes by hearing the word of God, the word of God as the Creator and Sustainer, whether in the sonorous phrases of Genesis chapter one, or the popular song, 'He's got the whole world in his hands.' The message is the same, and the call the same. Trust God and live.

2 THE IDEAL LIFE

Genesis 2.15 (NEB) 'The Lord God took the man and put him in the garden of Eden'

1 The garden

Is this true? Is the place into which man has been introduced on being born into this world really like a garden? Would this be the description that would spring to the mind of the urchins whom Borrelli cared for in the back streets of Naples? And what about the concrete jungle of our modern mammoth connurbations? Again, do the Gorbels in Glasgow in any sense resemble a garden? Yet such is the environment into which the lives of thousands upon thousands of people have been cast. Was then this Yahwistic theologian (as the scholars call him) who wrote Genesis chapter two a hopeless romantic, out of touch with life as it really is? Or could it be that the natural order God has provided for man does compare with a garden, but man has made a mess of it? Old prints of the countryside in Lambeth south of the River Thames compared with the present legacy of the industrial revolution make it appear so.

There is more to an ideal life, however, than a garden-like environment. Have not many retired people learnt this the hard way? During their annual holidays in Devon and Cornwall, fastening their eyes on the glories of the open sea after the confinement of some industrial city in the North of England, they have reckoned that to spend their retirement in such a place would be heaven itself—but it isn't. There is more truth in the caustic comment, 'You can only live on a view for a fortnight.' Other requirements are necessary to make for a happy life in addition to a garden-like environment, and Genesis chapter two tells us what they are.

2 Four necessities

First, work. Genesis expresses this bluntly—'The Lord God took the man and put him in the garden of Eden to till it and

4

care for it.' We have largely lost this conception of work today. Too often work is regarded as an evil, and the only sensible attitude with regard to it is to press for shorter hours. This is a mistake. The ideal life consists in satisfying work done for its own sake.

Secondly, freedom. 'You may eat from every tree in the garden' is the permission given to man. No one is happy surrounded by fences. He must have scope for the development of his skills, and if this includes investigating the surface of the moon, the summit of the Himalayas, or the structure of the atom, it must be granted. The garden called the universe is for man to explore, his happiness requires it.

Thirdly, a surprising necessity, surprising because apparently at odds with the freedom already insisted on—there must be a prohibition. So 'no holds barred', is not the description of the ideal life after all! But wait; the prohibition is necessary so that liberty shall not run out into licence. Absolute freedom is an impossibility. If all the plants in the garden are allowed to grow where they will, the garden will soon cease to be a garden, and will become a wilderness. Freedom, therefore, so necessary for the ideal life, must have checks and this is provided by the sovereignty of God. Man is free, but free under God, not in independence of him.

Fourthly, man needs fellowship. 'It is not good for man to be alone', says this passage from Genesis. He cannot develop in isolation and he cannot be happy without a community. The animal world provides company, but without language, and the latter is essential for full partnership for language is the instrument of fellowship. We do not only require a beautiful garden in which to live, we need people with whom we can talk.

APPEAL

What, therefore, must we do? We must concern ourselves with our environment. We must make war on all ugliness, slum dwellings and dirt. But we must remember all the time that glass and concrete, central heating and freezers, do not ensure happiness. The ideal life does not consist in reclining in a beautiful garden some one else has prepared. We need satisfying work which may involve blood, sweat, toil and tears. We need freedom to move and discipline as a safeguard. We also need people around us with whom we can converse and share our experiences. 'The Lord God took man and put him in the garden . . . ' but he had to keep the garden himself, and woe betide him if he did not give his mind to it.

3 OUTSIDE THE GARDEN

Genesis 3.23 (NEB) *'So the Lord God drove him out of the garden of Eden . . . '*

INTRODUCTION

We sat opposite each other at dinner sharing a small table. But we were not together. I had no idea who my fellow-traveller was on the fast train from the North to London, except that she was a good looking young woman, possibly in her thirties. I felt I had to speak. It seemed churlish not to do so, since we should be opposite each other for quite an hour. I led in therefore with a non-committal comment on the railway strike reported in the evening paper as all set for the next day. She took it seriously, even sadly, I thought. Then I discovered that she was a Trade Union official returning home from tough negotiations. She was disillusioned, not only I gathered, about the particular problem on which she had been engaged, but disillusioned about the whole of the hard and self-sacrificing labour she had put into her calling, because for her it was a calling. She worked not for the rewards of her office but for the welfare of the community for which she cared. What was hurting her was the apparent fact that in spite of all the improvements of the last decades, the solution of our social and community problems seemed as remote as ever. As soon as we righted one wrong, another appeared and discontent was widespread. Could it be, perhaps, that the root of our troubles lay in the hearts of people rather more than in the conditions in which they worked? We talked till we reached King's Cross, then I saw her no more.

1 Disillusionment

Could it be that the writer of Genesis chapter three had been a disillusioned man? Had he, perhaps, witnessed some family or some township where all the conditions for a happy communal life seemed set fair and yet a wholesome life eluded them? How has it come about that the fall of man, as we call it in theological circles, or the failure of man to make a success of his life—how has it come about that this is described as taking place in a perfect environment? For let us be certain of this, the story of Adam and Eve in the garden of Eden is not a description of past historical events, but an analysis of the perennial experience of men and women everywhere. Genesis three is almost harsh in its diagnosis. It says, even though men be placed in a perfect environment arranged by God himself, success does not follow. What an indictment of the nature of man! What pessimism! Or is it realism?

We do not like this scripture, indeed, if there are any remnants of the nineteenth century idea of inevitable progress left in our minds, we hate it. We prefer to imagine that mankind is marching forward, in spite of set-backs, toward the uplands of a brave new world. Man has achieved so much, what is there he cannot achieve?

Close to the beginning of the Old Testament, however, is set this story of man's rebellion against the sovereignty of God. That is to say, scarcely has it proclaimed its message that God is supreme, than it comes in with the statement that man will not have it so. Man therefore lives under the judgement of God, he does not enjoy the garden God has provided, indeed, he is expelled from it. What could be more terse than the words of verse 27 of this famous chapter, 'So the Lord God drove him out of the garden of Eden . . .'

2 The theological prologue

All this constitutes the theological prologue of the Old Testament. It says in effect, you will not penetrate to the heart of the story we are about to tell, the story of the Hebrew people, beginning with Abraham, Isaac and Jacob, and running on for a thousand years or more, only to end in abject failure concerning which there is nothing edifying to say, you will be baffled by it unless you are prepared to read it through the eyes of this theology that God has created a glorious world, but men have rebelled against his sovereignty, reaping in themselves the reward of disappointment, meaninglessness and sorrow.

3 God's solution

But there is a solution. God indeed has provided the solution. He is a God of judgement, but also a God of mercy. It was a theme sufficient to kindle the poetry of Psalm 101, a subject to sing about. 'My song shall be of mercy and judgement: unto thee O Lord will I sing.' The story which begins with Abraham is the story of God's provision for bringing men back into the garden. This way is the way of faith, the way of belonging, to a people *and* to a land, and expressing thankfulness for God's deliverances through the obedience of worship and social justice. In other words, the Old Testament is the story of God's sovereignty, man's rebellion and God's moves in history to win him back, all of which points still to permanent truth. God is still seeking man outside his garden, and the glory of the New Testament is that his Son, the Lord Christ, actually went outside himself to find him there.

4 LAW AND ORDER

Genesis 8.22 (NEB)

> 'While the earth lasts
> seedtime and harvest, cold and heat,
> summer and winter, day and night,
> shall never cease.'

We take it for granted. It is inconceivable to us that the sun might not rise at a certain time tomorrow and set at an equally certain time. Have we not the hours and the minutes listed in our diaries? There simply cannot be two nights running without an interval of daylight. How could it be possible unless of course the earth ceased to rotate on its axis? Similarly, there cannot be two winters running, because the earth is in orbit around the sun. So we have seedtime and harvest, cold and heat, summer and winter, day and night. It stands to reason! But does it? Only because law and order are built into nature making it a system.

1 Embedded law and order

This then is one of the first messages of the preaching from the Old Testament, that law is embedded in nature, and that nature is embedded in law. It is new preaching. Such thinking did not belong to Israel's neighbours. For them, as for polytheism generally, existence depended on the whim of the gods. What the Old Testament distinctively preaches needs, however, to be heard now. Of course we believe it in the physics laboratory! How could physics, or any other science, proceed unless it accepted a principle of regularity in the object of its investigation? But do we accept it in the sphere of human behaviour? Do we believe that one set of actions leads to disaster, and another set of actions, leads to well-being? Or can we stand all moral distinctions on their heads? Permissiveness suggests that we can. Anything goes. But does it? Not according to the Old Testament. There is a built-in law and order in the created universe which we

9

reverse at our peril. 'They have sown the wind, they shall reap the whirlwind', cried Hosea (8.7), concerning the faithless Northern Israel. The Creator's laws are no less inexorable for not being imposed either arbitrarily or from on high. They run through every creature's being, no one can successfully evade them.

2 *Formation necessitates law*

We return to the text.

> 'While the earth lasts
> seedtime and harvest, cold and heat,
> summer and winter, day and night,
> shall never cease.'

It suggests growth. Not for nothing is it frequently employed for Harvest Thanksgiving sermons. And how fitting that Bultmann chose this text for a powerful sermon on March 9th 1937, when the spring had pushed away the last remnants of a particularly depressing winter from the German countryside. But growth is never haphazard. It proceeds with rhythm. It is controlled by built-in law. All formation requires order and form implies shape. This does not only obtain in the physical sphere but in the personal. A people advancing to nationhood must be shaped, and discipline must do the shaping, even if freely accepted. So the Hebrew people, rescued from the tyranny of Egypt under Moses, as a rabble, were at once offered the law at Sinai in order that they might be formed or shaped into a nation. Formation and shaping necessitate law and order and not only at the national level, but also at the family and individual level. Jimmy must be trained to wash behind his ears. Mary has to be ordered to clean her teeth. Discipline is necessary until habits are formed, which then proceed with their own discipline, and so form is kept. These are the considerations the current permissiveness has discarded, and in doing so has jeopardised development, till in the end permissiveness and formlessness are seen to accompany each other because the one is the corollary of the other. The permissive are generally untidy.

Therefore the Old Testament preaches a gospel of law and order. It preaches it so that the nation and the individual may be formed or shaped. This is the Old Testament's distinctive *kerygma*, the kernel of it is the ten commandments, which no growing individual, no advancing nation, can abandon successfully and mature.

3 Law and grace

We must note, however, that although God gives the laws, the giving is an act of grace. In the book of Genesis where our text occurs—'While the earth lasts seedtime and harvest ... shall never cease'—it stands as a promise that the flood which resulted in the destruction of life will never recur. God's laws have a gracious purpose. They are designed to preserve. No society, therefore, which hopes to live, nor even the Church, can with impunity abandon or undermine them. Grace and faith must of course be dominant in the Church, but there must also be order, which means not only the ten commandments retained in use, but also structures and patterns in life and worship, together with discipline.

Law cannot, however, have the final word and for this reason, that men's formation and society's formation are unsafe. They are permanently unsafe because men are sinners. It is embedded in our natures to break laws. Therefore we need to be transformed as well as formed, indeed, transformation needs to complete our formation. This is the preaching of the New Testament. It mediates the gospel of Jesus Christ calling for faith in him. Nevertheless what is transformed must first be formed. Therefore law and order are never obsolete. The gospel of Christ does not invalidate them, and the Old Testament preaching is never out of date. Law and order stand as God's gift to men and women, by which they are made happier than they would be without them. They are designed for our growth, for our preservation and for our safety. It is God's will that they shall never cease.

5 THE GOSPEL OF THE LAND

Genesis 12.7 'I give this land to your descendants'

In Britain during the early nineteenth century agriculture suffered a period of acute depression. If not wholly caused by, it was certainly aggravated by, the industrial revolution wherein energetic and thrusting men forged ahead making money. So masses of people emigrated, or were driven from the land to the towns. This was the beginning of trouble. From then on rootlessness became a feature of industrialisation debasing personal and communal life. It still carries this penalty and in this respect there is little to choose between Düsseldorf, Turin, Lille or Detroit. And with the export of industrialisation from the western lands to Africa and the Far East, there has gone too the curse of rootlessness.

The Old Testament is opposed to rootlessness. In its place it preaches a gospel of the land, a place where people can be rooted, where they can enjoy the satisfaction of belonging, and by means of which there is something to pass on to the people that follow after. According to the Old Testament man needs a land in order to be safe, if not saved. He is unable to develop in a wholesome fashion bodily, mentally and spiritually unless he belongs somewhere. He has to belong to a people. He has also to belong to a land. And so the Old Testament is not content to tell only of God's peculiar, that is God's special people (Exodus 19.5), and how safety lay in belonging to them, it also tells of God's promise of a land, indeed even before Israel was formed into a self-conscious nation, there was made the promise to Abraham, the father of the Hebrew people, 'I will give this land to your descendants', crying aloud the message that a land is needed for man's salvation. Moreover, so frequently does the word land occur in the Old Testament, that he would need to be a diligent student to count how many times, and even then he would not begin to feel its emotive force unless he were an Israeli and could pronounce it in Hebrew, *HA-AREZ*. With all the depth of significance of the land, no wonder the Jews felt the exile in Babylon to be almost unbearable, and the

Diaspora hardly less so. In losing their land they had to struggle not to believe that they had lost their salvation. Perhaps man does not have to be a Jew to experience something of the pull of his homeland or why did that Australian write so poignantly the other day to Somerset House, London, pleading with its officers, if they cared for a fellow human being at all, to try and trace out for him how he came to be born in India of English parents of whom he could find no records at all. He needed to know to what land he belonged.

If then the Old Testament's message that for his personal wholesomeness man needs a land, is true, what corollaries are there for our present time? Perhaps there are three.

1 *Patriotism*

First, there is a danger in despising patriotism. This does not mean danger primarily on military considerations, but danger to the health of a community. Of course Edith Cavell was right when she said in 1915, 'Patriotism is not enough', but patriotism is still required, because if it is rejected, it carries with it the deprivation of roots. A plant needs roots. A people needs roots. An individual needs roots. Furthermore, a plant needs roots in a certain place, probably in the confined and shallow space of a seed-tray carefully set in a sheltered position and nurtured. Likewise a people needs to be rooted in a family, a community and a nation. It cannot begin its life by being rooted in humanity, or the northern hemisphere, or the white races. It is to be hoped that there will come development into this breadth of belonging. Even so, no living organism can stay alive without its roots. This is why patriotism is essential. Not of the kind that is called jingoism, nor blind patriotism (my country right or wrong), but patriotism that sees the faults in one's own people and yet seeks its welfare, not shrinking from sacrifice, nor failing to intercede with God on its behalf. Jesus was sufficiently patriotic to weep over his nation's blindness. If the Old Testament is right when it affirms that for its safety a people needs a land, abjuring rootlessness, we cannot banish patriotism.

2 Conservation

Secondly, we must take the conservation of earth's natural resources seriously. When God, in the words of the Old Testament promised the Hebrews a land, he promised a land 'flowing with milk and honey', that is, a productive land, a land in complete contrast to the desert they had endured for forty years. Modern man's technological expertise has produced a land in the Western world flowing with milk and honey, but unless he abandons his greedy exploitation of earth's natural resources, he will turn it back into a desert. Signs are not wanting of fertile lands reverting to dust bowls, seas gutted of fish, spring dawns almost silent of song, because the birds have been starved out by insecticides. Exploitation with no concern but for profit is not only foolish but sinful. It is destroying one of the means of God's provision for man's safety—the land.

3 The call to beautify

Thirdly, there is a call to beautify. At the present time the message impinges most upon those responsible for our towns and cities. Here it is only fair to record that in some areas of the heaviest industrial concentration in the north of England, there is growing up a welcome civic pride upgrading city centres almost beyond recognition. Cities like Sheffield, Bradford and Dewsbury have done wonders. In all this the Clean Air Bill and the campaign against the pollution of the environment deserve widespread support. At the same time it must be said that we are witnessing the spoilation of too many places of architectural merit, like Lincoln, Aberdeen, Bristol and Salisbury. A book called The Rape of Britain, published in June 1975, sets out with depressing illustrations the soulless buildings that have been erected in the second half of the twentieth century, by unimaginative planning. And if the developers are chiefly to blame, those who granted the permission, and our modern architects, are not wholly without a charge against them. The environment has an effect on the lives of the people who live in it. There is something dispiriting about living in the proximity of highrise blocks, let alone inside them, and man needs spirit, he cannot afford to have it crushed out of him by a cold, cruel, concrete wilderness. What is needed is every conceivable effort to beautify as far as possible even the cityscape. We neglect it at our peril. Every person indeed who owns a patch of ground should 'doll it up' as best he can. This is the implication from the preaching of the Old Testament that God promised his people a 'goodly land'.

Is this concern for the environment only a matter for governments and local authorities? But what about that block of flats where efforts were conspicuously lacking to beautify it till one family took a holiday in Switzerland and saw what the Swiss do with geraniums on the balconies of their chalets and even their railways stations! Why could not others accomplish the like? And they did. One balcony at least in that block blossomed with flowers, but not only one for long. The other tenants were not to be outdone. Soon the whole place was transformed. And who shall say that the occupants were not much happier people as a result of their achievement. This is the gospel of the land. It is the message of the Old Testament preaching. It is preaching we do well to hear.

6 PRAYERFUL LIVING

Genesis 24.12 'And he said, "O Lord, the God of my master Abraham, send me, I pray thee, good speed this day, and show kindness unto my master Abraham".'

I ask you to imagine a large, deep hole in the earth with steps leading down to the water which is bubbling up from the spring that is there. At the top of the steps is a large trough empty of water and close by it a man at the head of a train of ten camels praying. If you listen you can hear his prayer: 'O Lord God ... send me, I pray thee, good speed this day, and show kindness unto my master Abraham. Behold, I stand by the fountain of water; and the daughters of the men of the city come out to draw water: and let it come to pass, that the girl to whom I shall say, "Let down thy pitcher, I pray thee, that I may drink'" and she shall say, "Drink, and I will give thy camels drink also": let the same be she that thou hast appointed for thy servant Isaac, and thereby I shall know that thou hast showed kindness unto my master.'

1 *God addressed*

Do you ever pray like that? No, I do not mean standing by a train of ten camels at a spring of water outside a city wall in Mesopotamia. I mean, do you ever pray about affairs of human interest like that? Do you ever pray for God's clear guidance expecting that he will show you what to do? Do you wait until his signs are clear? Because these are the points in this man's praying of whom I have drawn you the sketchiest of pictures but which is all filled out in one of the longest picture stories in Genesis, namely, chapter 24. This man was seeking a wife for his master's son. Surely there can be nothing more human than choosing a wife, nothing more domestic, but he prayed about it. Perhaps it is a pity men and women don't pray more than they do about the partners sought in marriage. . . .

And then if you look you can see a sight to take your breath away. Out through the city gate there comes a woman, young, beautiful and stately. The Orient has few scenes more captivating than veiled women making for the well, their water-pots poised upon their steady heads. And to add perfection to the scene this one was fair. Here was enough to make a praying man stop praying. And he did, not from distraction, but from overwhelming attraction. Could this be the answer to his prayer? She went down to the water. She filled her pitcher. She re-ascended the steps. The praying man could withold himself no longer, he ran to meet her. Could this be the woman, the woman for his master's son?

Trembling, he let the test words slip from his lips: 'Give me to drink, I pray thee, a little water of thy pitcher!'

I am sure I am addressing no one who has had no experience of tense moments in his life, no one who has not, for instance, held a letter in his hand wondering, 'Shall I open it?' knowing that when he does, his destiny is settled. Such occasions come to us all; breathless, we await the outcome. So did this man that evening by his train of ten camels and the empty water trough. Had the girl replied 'no' to his request for water, all his confidence in the promises of God might well have lain shattered before his eyes, but if she said 'yes', he would feel a very humble man in the presence of the great eternal God who answers prayer. Remember, he had crossed hundreds of miles of pitiless desert for a moment such as this.

2 God's answer

What did she say, that girl, I mean, standing there at the top of the steps with her pitcher full upon her head? She said, ' "Drink, my Lord:" and she hasted and let down her pitcher upon her hand, and gave him to drink.' And then this, ' "I will draw water for thy camels also until they have done drinking." And she hasted and emptied her pitcher into the trough, and ran again to the well to draw, to draw for all the camels.'

Have you ever seen a camel drink? You wonder when, if ever, it will stop. This girl filled up that water trough with her pitcher and every filling meant a journey up and down those tiring steps, till every beast was satisfied.

There is in one of the collects in our prayer book this phrase about God, 'who is wont to give more than either we desire or deserve.' This praying man by the water trough knew nothing of the collects from the *Book of Common Prayer*, but had he known, he would have said his 'Amen' loud and clear. He asked for a sign and he received more than he asked. 'Drink,' she said, 'I will draw water for thy camels also until they have done drinking.' She filled the water trough herself.

3 God's concern

Religion for too many people has become a subject for argument instead of an instrument by which to live. Of course there has to be ecclesiastical organization but it is best if hidden away like the works under the bonnet of a car instead of displayed for the boredom of the many. And rational considerations have to be applied to our religion or it runs out in a morass of dangerous supersition; but religion is not ecclesiology nor theology, nor philosophical enquiry, important as is the part each one has to play. The only religion with survival value is a practical way of life, believing in God in such a way that we rely on him, and commune with him, and look for guidance from him, even in the day-to-day concerns of everyday life.

Here is a man sitting behind a desk, his pen poised in his hand over a letter his secretary has placed before him. No one peering into that room could have guessed the seriousness of the situation. No voices were raised, few words were spoken and they only monosyllabic. But the man with the pen knew of the agony that lay behind the drafting of that letter. He understood the risks that were being run, and he was aware of the repercussions there could be on the other side of the world when that letter reached its destination. Was it surprising that in the moment before he appended his signature he raised his heart in a quick prayer to God? Is not this what we do, all of us, when we are up against it? Ask the people suddenly confronted by a hijacker in an aircraft! Sound out a prisoner of war being led out for interrogation! Not long ago some research was made into this aspect of religion and the surprising result indicated that some seventy per cent of all men apparently engage in this kind of practical belief in God, and some fifty per cent of women. It seems that the majority make a reference to God at times. When we have done everything that we can we place the issue in the hands of Another. In a crisis it is rational to pray, and the Bible does not condemn us for doing so.

The book of Genesis is deceptively simple. In actual fact it handles the fundamental questions about existence, not least in the introductory first eleven chapters. Here is thinking driven so far into the timeless that it can only be expressed succinctly in symbolic form. But the things by which we live are not only answers to ultimate questions but love and home and people to care about. The book of Genesis therefore makes no blunder into naïveté, when it goes on to tell of a man seeking a wife for his master and praying about the matter. Chapter 24 of Genesis is not a mistake. God is shown here as answering prayer, and not only prayer about Church Synods and Her Majesty's government, but prayer about domestic matters. God is a Father. God is our Father. A father is concerned about his children's every-day needs. The awareness of this was basic in the life of Jesus. Let us be careful then not to be cheated out of the consolations of religion by sophistication. We need consolation at times, and prayer concerning the supposed commonplaces of life is not improper. Let today's Bible story contribute to our encouragement. Then it is no antiquarian scripture but rather a word of God and an incentive to daily prayerful living.

7 WHAT SORT OF GOD?

Exodus 3.6 (NEB) *'I am . . . the God of Abraham, the God of Isaac, the God of Jacob.'*

It rolls off the tongue—'I am . . . the God of Abraham, the God of Isaac, the God of Jacob' ringing like a formula or incantation. It belongs to that category of phrase which is heard but rarely listened to, and certainly not analysed. But suppose we do, suppose we cup our hands over our ears and listen attentively, then the words are sufficient to make us start. That God should admit to being the God of any one of these three men, that he should, in a sense, own them, is surprising enough, but when he proclaims himself as the God of all three together, the comment 'fantastic' is scarcely too strong.

1 *The God of individuals*

What sort of God does the Old Testament proclaim? It proclaims a God ready to own each man as he is, in all his stark individuality. Look at Abraham, Isaac and Jacob! There is no need to be dogmatic about their historicity, indeed, if we allocate these patriarchal stories to the category of saga, the message cries out the more. These men were acutely different from each other—but God owned the. Abraham with his thrusting, enquiring, extrovert nature; Isaac with his retreating, reflective, introvert personality; Jacob, devious, grasping and sensitive. Not one of them an 'oil-painting.' Abraham could lie like the next man to save his skin; Isaac was withdrawn to the point of weakness, a man who could not bestir himself even to choose his own wife; Jacob was up to any tricks that would turn affairs to his advantage. But God owned them, weaknesses, trickery and all! This is the kind of God the Old Testament proclaims, a God who owns Adam because he made him. Adam is mankind, but not only mankind, he is you with your peculiarities, me with my peculiarities, that man whose pigmented skin and way of thinking is so different from mine, even to the point of being alien, and that woman next door whose temperament I can barely understand. 'I am the God of Abraham, the God of Isaac, the God of Jacob.' 'I am the God of Augustine and Pelagius, Luther and Erasmus, Calvin and Arminius, General Booth and Pope John, Billy Graham and Archbishop Ramsey.' God owns us not in spite of our differences, but because of our differences, for his creations are not standardized, they make up an infinite variety; which means you are significant not because you are like the next man, but because you are different from him. There are no copies and no repeats when it comes to people. Everyone is different, even to his finger-prints. 'Look at this', says the collector of precious stones, holding a ruby in the palm of his hand, 'have you ever seen the like?' So is the God whom the Old Testament proclaims, he treasures each one for his individuality. 'I am the God of Abraham, the God of Isaac, the God of Jacob.' It is a gospel for contemporary standardized man!

2 *The God of the Church*

God owned these three individuals, but he owned them together. And not only did he own them as a trio, he owned them as the patriarch or forefather of a community. Abraham, Isaac and Jacob supremely belonged to the Hebrew people, and the Hebrew people supremely belonged to Abraham, Isaac and Jacob. The God whom the Old Testament proclaims is the God of the community, the God of a nation, the God of Israel. It is not for our safety that we remain as individuals separate from God, it is not even for our safety that we may remain as individuals, each one united to God by our own personal and individual confession of faith, we must join hands with our fellow believers and confess 'I am the God of Abraham, the God of Isaac, the God of Jacob' together. This is what every individual must do who would be safe—recognise the differences in his neighbour and accept him all the same. That man who glories in 'pop' music, and that man who cannot stand it. That woman who is never so happy as when knee-deep in a kitchen, and that woman who prefers to study fossils in the Natural History Museum. We are all different but we shall not be safe, that is to say, we shall not be wholesome, unless we recognize that we belong together. And to help us realise this, God called out the Old Israel and God called out the New Israel, the Church, in which we are bound to accept each other as also belonging. This is why a comprehensive Church, a universal Church, and a catholic Church, is proper, and all that makes for sectarianism is improper. God owns Abraham, Isaac and Jacob together, and Abraham, Isaac and Jacob together must admit their faith in God. It is in the light of this that Church unity and the unity of mankind become imperative.

3 *The God of History*

And now a third point. The God whom the Old Testament proclaims is a God of history. 'I am the God of your forefathers, the God of Abraham, the God of Isaac, the God of Jacob.' This is what Moses heard at the place of the burning bush in Sinai when he felt himself summoned to the leadership of the Hebrew people, charged with bringing them out of the slavery of Egypt into a new status of nationhood with a land of their own. Four times over in chapter three of the book of Exodus this phrase rings like a bell, 'I am the God of your forefathers . . . ' There is continuity in God's dealings with men. The God whom the Old Testament proclaims is no capricious God who acts impulsively out of anger or love. He has a purpose, a plan, and an end in view; and when he owns individuals, be they as unlike as Abraham, Isaac and Jacob, or when he calls a whole people, be it the nation of Israel, the Church, or any other community, it is always to take part in his health-giving design for mankind; or if we must resort to a theological phrase—*election* for service within God's overall purpose.

And now we feel abandoned in the presence of high sounding generalities. But need we be? There are few experiences more hurting in life than to sense that we are unwanted, that it would not really matter if we failed in our work or gloriously succeeded, that everything comes to the same in the end whether we lie and cheat, fornicate and embezzle, no one is better off for struggling along the hard way of honesty in life—indeed, what advantage or disadvantage would there be if we did not exist at all? Pointlessness drains away the vitality of our beings. But the Old Testament says no. God is working out his purpose in history, he has called your forebears to take part in that purpose and now he is calling your generation. And not only you as an individual within your generation, but your church (yes, your little church, struggling to pay its way in a time of inflation), and your nation. We may of course refuse. Even so, we may still be taken up into the purposes of God as was Pharaoh in the book of Exodus, and Ahaz in the book of Isaiah; but if we co-operate, if we own the God who owns us, our little life's history is taken up in God's grand design in history. This is the faith that buoyed up Israel. This is what made these people 'tick'. It is doubtful if any people, any person, is able to rise to his full stature lacking a sense of destiny, a sense which develops when we hear God proclaimed as the God of history. 'I am the God of your forefathers, the God of Abraham, the God of Isaac, the God of Jacob', and we respond.

4 *The contemporary God*

But there are always today's pressing concerns and tomorrow's uncertainties. It falls to very few men to be able to sit down and philosophise, and to far less women. There is that business contract to be registered, the children's schooling to be decided, tomorrow's inflated grocery bill to be settled, and the house mortgage to be borne. This plus the increased area in which 'do-it-yourself' has now become a necessity, leaves little time for assessing God's hand in history, even if it is visible at all. But wait a minute! Where was God shown as the God of this people's forefathers, the God of Abraham, the God of Isaac, the God of Jacob? It was when the heart-rending cry of a whole nation was ringing insistently in a man's ears. It was when his fellow-country men were pouring out their life's strength under the lash of taskmaster's whips to satisfy the ambition of a foreign tyrannical ruler. It was when young women were choking back their cries as they saw their male children tossed by order in the Nile. There is no incentive for philosophising in conditions like these, no incentive where life consists in a struggle for existence. When a people has lost its liberty it has no stomach for more than tomorrow's task. So what sort of God is of use in conditions like these? What kind of God is of value for a man summoned to lead such people out of bondage into the freedom of a promised land? Only a God who is sufficient for each day's emergency as it arises, a God whose being cannot be comprehended in a formula, label or name, but a God who is proved in experience to be adequate for all human needs, if only we dare to trust him. This is what the God of the Old Testament proclaimed himself to be, in the ears of Moses burdened by his peoples' slavery to contemporary tasks. 'I will be what I will be'. God is he who meets people at the point of their need, whatever it is.

Who then can this be but the living God? And is not this precisely how Jesus read this scripture? Retorting to the cynical question of the Sadducees concerning the resurrection, in which they did not believe, confining themselves safely, or so they thought, in their agnosticism, to the Pentateuch as their canon of Scripture. But Jesus reverted to that same portion of the Old Testament to proclaim God as the living God, 'Have you never read what God himself said to you: "I am the God of Abraham, the God of Isaac, and the God of Jacob"? He is not the God of the dead but of the living' (Matthew 22.32) God is not dead. This has always been axiomatic for the Jews. God is the living God. God is active in history. God is the one who meets contemporary needs. This is the very heart of Old Testament preaching.

When you sit at your desk tomorrow, or work in your kitchen, or stand at your laboratory bench, your mind necessarily occupied with your work in hand, you may know that you count in life just because you are you. You count to God and you count to the community in which you live. Do not refuse to believe this in the days when you feel a failure or when the problems facing our generation seem beyond our ability to solve them. God is the God of Abraham, the God of Isaac, and the God of Jacob. This makes all the difference.

8 GOD'S PECULIAR

Exodus 19.5 ' . . . ye shall be a peculiar treasure unto me from among all peoples.'

Everyone or almost everyone in the English speaking world is acquainted with Westminster Abbey. That is to say, everyone at least knows where it is, probably what it looks like, and almost certainly everyone is aware of its overriding significance in English history as the place where the kings and queens have been crowned since the days of William the Conqueror. But how many people know that when a great service takes place there, it is not the Archbishop of Canterbury who pronounces the final blessing, but the Dean? This is because Westminster Abbey is a 'royal peculiar' and no Bishop, or even Archbishop, exercises authority over it. Like St George's Chapel, Windsor, Westminster Abbey owes its final allegiance directly to the Crown. This is what makes it 'a royal peculiar'.

1 God's peculiar

In the Old Testament we encounter a different kind of peculiar—God's peculiar, or as the New English Bible expresses Exodus 19.5, God's 'special possession.' The reference is to a nation, God's peculiar people. This is what the Hebrews were called to be, a status first acquired when they found themselves slaves in Egypt, pouring out their life blood in labour gangs to serve the pride of the Pharaohs, a bondage from which they escaped through the Red Sea (or Sea of Reeds) into the Sinai desert, perhaps about the year 1225 B.C.

There is a sense in which every nation is a peculiar people, a fact which has witness borne to it in the Old Testament itself (Amos 9.7). Is it not true that the French are unlike the Germans and the Germans are unlike the Japanese? Each ethnic group has its peculiar contribution to make to the totality of mankind. The unique feature of the Hebrew people, however, lay in the recognition which it came to acquire that God had called them out of Egypt, God had led them through the Red Sea, God had prepared a way for them into the land of Canaan, which therefore acquired the title 'the promised land'. These convictions about God's choice of their nation formed the basis of Israel's creed and out of it there grew a way of life embodied in what is called 'the Covenant'. Exodus chapter 19 expresses this with the utmost clarity. 'Ye have seen what I did unto the Egyptians, and how I bare you on eagles' wings, and brought you unto myself. Now therefore, if ye will obey my voice indeed, and keep my covenant, then ye shall be a peculiar treasure unto me from among all peoples: for all the earth is mine.' So the peculiar way of life the Hebrews kept constituted their perennial witness to their belief that God had called them into being.

2 Israel's burden

Did the Hebrews enjoy being God's peculiar? Does privilege invariably carry total satisfaction? Then why do public schoolboys affect the clothes of manual workmen? And why do some peers campaign to be free of their titles? The truth is, there are embarrassments for the sensitive in being different. We may be sure that the Hebrews were not wholly uniformly proud of being different from other nations which surrounded them; different in their worship, different in their morals, different in their customs, different in their clothes, different in their homes, different from the time they arose in the morning till the time they went to bed at night—do you think they enjoyed being peculiar? Some of them did. They gloried in their strangeness. It made them proud of their pedigree, proud of their accomplishments (which were, and are, considerable), and proud of their special status before God. But not all reacted in this fashion. Perhaps very few of them consistently reacted in this fashion. Being God's peculiar became in fact 'a burden grievous to be borne', and more than half the story of the Hebrew people is the story of how they tried to slough off their uniqueness to live like ordinary people.

Hear them, for instance, on one occasion, crying out to their prophet Samuel—'Appoint us a king to govern us, like other nations' (Samuel 8.5 NEB). Witness, too, King Solomon erecting his costly temple and his costly palace ostentatious with costly ornamentation, grinding down his subjects in sweated labour, all to create an impression equal to or even superior to that of all the nations round about. See also Ahab, king of northern Israel, forging his foreign alliances and conducting his aggressive wars, acting indeed like any other petty royalty. And Ahaz, king of Judah, copying even the heathen altar he admired in Assyria and setting it up in Jerusalem as a place of sanctity.

Is it not true that throughout its long history Israel lived under the tension of loving to be God's peculiar and hating to be God's peculiar; now enjoying being different, now loathing being different; now relying for protection on the God who delivered them out of Egypt, now trusting their own political sagacity and military expertise—and never succeeding in either! This is the tragedy of the history of Israel, that this people was called to be God's peculiar and never ceased attempting to escape from the corresponding weight this responsibility entailed.

It is a story which makes us ask the question, why? Why did God choose a nation? Why was such a heavy load laid upon such a little people? What was God's aim? What was God's purpose? And the answer is—so that there might be a permanent question mark written across man's age-long attempt to organise all life without a reference beyond himself. Self-centredness, propulsion by uncontrolled instinct, reliance upon human ingenuity and expertise does result in ruin. So God willed 'to throw a spanner' in these humanistic works to make men think again. And so he brought on to the stage of history a non-conforming people, disturbing the audience to ask some pointed questions leading thereby to the possibility of a return to wholesomeness.

3 The Church a peculiar

But this is history. What of the present? God's peculiar, Israel, remains for ever posing questions. There is however a new Israel, inheritors of the first; we call it the Church, the people of God. This also is God's peculiar. This also bears the burden of being God's question mark to the world, querying the tacit but widespread assumption that secularism is the only rational interpretation of human existence. There is no power beyond the human brain. There is no life beyond the here and now, no other dimension, no eternal Spirit, no miracle. The Church is called to question these assumptions, and to live a life which questions them, in other words, to act as God's 'non-conformists' in a materialistic society.

And now the hurting enquiries! Does the Church enjoy being a peculiar in contemporary society? Is not the urge strong within us all to conform? Shall we not (Church people) commend ourselves more in a Welfare State if we occupy ourselves supremely with welfare? And must we not, if we are to survive, accommodate our marriage discipline to the prevailing customs of our time? Where indeed shall we be with the young if we do not realign with the sexual mores of our time? Let us face it. The temptations are strong.

But are we sure that the Old Testament has no message for us today? Israel, of course, could be, has indeed been, too rigid as God's peculiar. The Church could be, indeed has been, too rigid as God's peculiar too. Nevertheless, unless old Israel, unless the new Israel, bears witness first by its worship, by its words and by its quality of life, to the existence of a dimension other than the human, the rational and the secular, it has no obvious raison d'être, it could as well be lost among the people of the world.

This in fact happened to the greater part of the Hebrew people. It conformed and it ceased to exist. Assyria overran the Northern Kingdom in war in 721 B.C., and for the most part these people were never seen again. And in 597 B.C., Babylon overran the kingdom of Judah deporting the cream of the nation into exile, and most of them likewise were never seen again—except that a small remnant returned more peculiar than ever and are identifiable as the *Ashkenazi* Jews of our day.

There is a spiritual risk in accepting the call of God to be his question mark in a secular age. It is separatism for separatism's sake, the classical label for which is Pharisaism, an unattractive exhibit. But there is a peril too in sloughing off this status. In the end it involves irreparable loss of indentity. Apart from its special calling Israel is insignificant, so is the Church. Its survival depends on its essential difference from its neighbours. Its strength lies in standing apart from its circumstances. According to so 'down-to-earth' a writer as is the anonymous author of the preface to Crockford's Clerical Directory 1975/6, the day is approaching, if it is not already upon us, when the Church will clearly be recognisable by its different standards of life from those which surround it. Some disclosure points are greed, idolatry, selfishness, violence, abortion-on-demand and easy divorce.

Is the call to be God's peculiar nothing but a burden? Westminster Abbey is a royal peculiar. Is there not a dignity attaching? So it is with the people of God. Membership lifts a man's head and straightens his back, supplying purpose and poise. And if we reckon it must minister pride, think again. Jesus was God's peculiar. In him Israel was summed up and we call the Church 'the body of Christ'. Christ surely was God's special possession, God's unique peculiar and he was never proud, never overbearing. Jesus was no kind of Pharisee.

9   THE TRANSMISSION OF A FAITH

Deuteronomy 26.4 (NEB) *'The priest shall take the basket from your hand and set it down before the altar of the Lord your God. Then you shall solemnly recite . . . "My father was a homeless Aramaean who went down to Egypt . . . But the Egyptians ill-treated us . . . Then we cried to the Lord the God of our fathers for help . . . and so the Lord brought us out of Egypt . . . and gave us this land." '*

Can you see this man? This man setting down his basket and reciting his confession of faith? Can you see his weather-beaten face? Can you see in imagination his rough hands? Do not make the mistake of reckoning that he would cheerfully abandon his action because he appears self-conscious in his best clothes and awkward making that set speech. This is one of the significant moments of his life, and he knows it. The fact that he performs this ceremony annually does not detract from the occasion. It underlines its importance and provides not only a pattern but a purpose for his life.

When I was in charge of a Church in north west London, we used to organise a Harvest Thanksgiving service. There was nothing unusual in it, but the decision had a measure of unreality in that built-up area, because the only way harvest produce could be forthcoming for decoration of the Church was to purchase it in the local shops. For one man, however, the occasion was significant. He was a retired chauffeur who lived in a mews flat which, from his point of view, was conveniently situated next to the railway. This provided a strip of land which the Railway Company allowed him to cultivate. So grateful was he for this that every year his priority on the allotment was to grow the biggest and most perfect marrow possible, and to bring it to our Harvest Thanksgiving service. For my first year there I received this marrow unceremoniously without realising how I was failing him. It was up to me, I saw, to arrange a time when he could bring his marrow (which meant putting on a suit, collar and tie), and I would lift it from his basket, examine it, compliment him on its size and shape, hear something of its growth history and then set it down reverently in the Church itself. Unfortunately he had no set piece to recite, but invariably he would say something about God's goodness throughout another year. This constituted his confession of faith.

1 *A cultus*

In this second half of the twentieth century thinking people have been asking themselves how religious faith can be transmitted from one generation to another. The question is important because if a nation ceases to believe in anything, it ceases to have a sense of purpose, and if it ceases to have a sense of purpose life falls apart, which is what we are beginning to see happen. The Old Testament presents an answer. Faith is transmitted by means of organised worship, a system which becomes traditional, is essentially enjoyable, and contains within it a confession of faith. This is what Deuteronomy chapter 26.1–11, the story of the man with his basket, advocates.

Not long ago I met a housewife who understood this principle. I was the preacher at the centenary celebrations of a church in the Black Country. She had two children, a boy and a girl, both under ten. They had been made to sleep in the afternoon so as to keep awake for the centenary celebrations in the evening. To these she added something for her own family, a special and memorable dinner party; for the boy a new suit and for the girl a new dress. That mother intended her two children to associate church with the happy things of life, so allowing the thought to crystalise in their minds that the continuance of a church and the faith it stood for, was something to be marked with joyfulness and thanksgiving; so they would receive it and so they would pass it on.

Festivals, when they become traditional, can become shows empty of faith content. This is a danger risked perhaps more in the Catholic wing of the church than the Protestant; nevertheless the Catholic approach has soundness in it. Faith is transmitted from generation to generation by means of set forms of traditional worship in which the community and the family have a part to play, and concerning which the children are bound to ask why. So Deuteronomy 6.20, 'When your son asks you in time to come, "What is the meaning of the precepts, statutes and laws . . . " you shall say to him, "We were Pharaoh's slaves in Egypt, and the Lord brought us out of Egypt with his strong hand . . . " ' Thus a confession of faith is provoked, giving the new generation a reason for its existence.

2 *The rejection of a cultus*

What of the present? What of the 1960s and 1970s? What attitude have we adopted to organised religion? What room have we for a cultus? The last two decades and more have witnessed its rejection. About the year 1960 attention was turned towards God's action in the secular. This was no plea for secularism, but it had the effect of diverting attention away from worship and concentrating instead on the service of mankind. So programmes of social welfare became the hall-mark of progressive Christians. At the same time across the Atlantic strident voices were announcing that 'God is dead', mystifying the man in the street by advertising 'a religionless Christianity'. All in all, for reasons good as well as bad, organised worship as a way of transmitting faith was hit hard, in some places almost to the point of demolition.

And now we are witnessing a different rejection. This belongs to the Pentecostalist or Charismatic movement. In this there is expressed a weariness with organised worship, not for the reason that secular Christianity wrote it off, but for the opposite reason. Worship in so far as it is organised cannot be a genuine expression of worship in the Spirit. What is required is spontaneity, sensation and feeling. The formal, the rational and the disciplined make little appeal to a generation wearied with the flatness of materialism. And so we have come to see movements like 'the Jesus movement' outside the established Churches, uninhibited, buoyant and formless, an approach in which it is claimed that the Spirit gives evident signs of his undoubted presence, which are the charismata or gifts of the Spirit.

All in all during the last decade and more, what Deuteronomy sees as the vehicle of faith, namely, organised worship, has suffered a heavy defeat, for which we may have to pay; such would seem to be the message of the Old Testament.

3 The need for a Spirit-filled cultus

What then is required? Has not Whitsuntide the answer? Whitsunday marked the birth of the organised Church and it marked the birth of the Spirit-filled Church. From that day the Church possessed an outreaching ministry, a message and a life-style recognizable by the general public. But it was no lifeless structure, it was pulsating with energy, flexible and joyous. Is there not here a word for us? We shall not transmit the Christian faith without forms of organised worship, sufficiently traditional to embody the principle of continuity; which is why too drastic reforms of the liturgy are self-defeating. We need patterns of worship that are colourful, joyful and therefore memorable, attracting to them popular customs which provoke the question 'why?' thus eliciting a confession of faith in simple terms.

But we need also room for the Spirit to enthuse and inspire. The Church needs a pentecostal movement as well as a cultus. The Old Testament bears witness to this. It had its priests but it also had its prophets and they worked together. Indeed neither can succeed without the other. Prophecy arose in the context of the cultus. This two-sidedness is essential. A Spirit-led Church alone can run to excess and dangerous eccentricity. A cultus-dominated Church can become fossilised and useless. The need of our time is for Spirit-filled organised worship, a paradox, no doubt, and a ground of tension, but paradox is no stranger in the Christian faith, and tension can be productive of good.

10 JUSTIFYING FAITH

Joshua 6.17 (NEB) 'No one is to be spared except the prostitute Rahab.'

Prostitution is not much of a profession. It has an ancient history, and there are prostitutes and prostitutes. A select few earn big money in the West End of London, but for the majority it is a sleazy underworld that they inhabit. Men are not wanting, of course, who justify this profession. Even some women, on other grounds, support its existence asserting that marriage remains tolerable if the husband has some outlet for his passion 'on the side'. Provided the prostitute can be kept in her place, which means out of sight, so the argument runs, society can accept, even be grateful for her existence.

Prostitution flourishes in time of war. The reasons are obvious. Soldiers are separated from their wives and from the sanctions of society they normally inhabit. Moreover, the possibility of death at any moment urges men forward to self-fulfilment with women. The women for their part, in a battle area are frequently desperate for the bare necessities of life. There is little prospect of gainful employment. The army alone has food. Husbands who provided for these women and protected them, have disappeared into the unknown, perhaps never to return. Somehow they must live. Somehow they have to provide for hungry children. It is not surprising that prostitution flourishes in time of war.

Prostitution is a dangerous profession. This is brought out by the Italian novelist Giulio Petroni's book called *La città calda*, in which he tells the story of two little Italian girls sidling up to a train-load of Italian troops being pulled out of the resistance the Germans were putting up to the advancing Americans. They were mere children, but as they climbed up on the buffers of the stationary cattle trucks in which the soldiers were locked, and peered through the slits in the planking, they soon learned that they were objects of interest and apparently had something to sell. As the story unwinds itself, the reader learns how they came to live by what they had to sell—themselves. But it was a dangerous world they inhabited. First, they gained their experience with the Italians, but as the Italians pulled farther and farther back from the battle zone, it was the Germans with whom they had to trade. And when these retreated, the Americans. In a situation like this prostitutes can readily be reckoned as spies by desperate soldiers. No one will ask questions if women who sell themselves for a cigarette are liquidated just in case . . . . But one of these girls lost her life for a different reason. Confident in her profession she mocked a soldier who proved to be incompetent. Maddened by her taunts he strangled her. Women who involve themselves with the passions of men run terrible risks. Prostitution operates in a dangerous world as well as a degrading one.

The Bible draws no curtains across this world. It is well aware of its existence and how it works. The Bible, especially the Old Testament, is realistic about human nature. It shows us people as they really are, as well as what they might be. In the Bible men and women fornicate, hate, murder and steal. This fact has been used as an argument in favour of the sale of pornographic literature. What these advocates choose to forget, however, is that if the Bible lets us see men fornicating, it also lets us see them turning away from it to serve the living God. When pornography begins to tell of a God of righteousness, mercy and judgement, will be the time for it to claim the Bible as on its side.

1 A house on the wall

Here, then, in the second chapter of the book of Joshua, we see two men secreting themselves through the city gate of Jericho, and making their way to the house of a prostitute named Rahab. It was located on the wall. They had no difficulty in finding it. A prostitute's house situated on a city wall manned by soldiers was convenient for them and for her. After all, where in any port or garrison town are the brothels located? And men in a brothel cause no eye-brows to be raised. Questions are not asked there. Clearly these two men who were spies of the Israelite armies besieging Jericho knew what they were about. They were more interested in the thickness of Jericho's walls and the troops manning them, than in Jericho's easy women. It was fortunate for them that this prostitute's house was actually on the outside wall overlooking the country beyond. From such a place they could feast their eyes on more than a woman.

But their luck wasn't in. Or was it? These two strangers had been spotted entering the city and traced to the house of Rahab the prostitute. At first light two emissaries of the king appeared before her door and demanded their extradition. 'But you are too late,' she said in effect, 'two men did visit me, but they left before midnight, where I do not know. Hurry, you may catch them.' This was a lie, a deliberate lie. The two men were at the time concealed on the roof among some stalks of flax which she had laid out in rows.

2 The revealing question

And now we ask the question, why? Why had this prostitute chosen to hide two Israelite spies? The whole point of the story being in the Bible at all is to be found in the answer to this question, why? It brings us down to the woman's motives, and motives for action are what interest the Bible, and what interests God. It is in fact on the basis of our motives rather than our achievements that God justifies or condemns us.

Why did this woman hide the spies? Because alongside carrying out her profession she had been thinking. She had been assessing the people around her, and she had been weighing carefully the reports that reached her ears from the soldiers whom she accommodated. Prostitutes learn secrets which is why they are a danger to security. Men talk in their weak moments and can be made to talk. Women know this and many trade on it. So Rahab learned how the Canaanite armies defending Jericho and other cities doubted their power to withstand the advancing Israelite armies. 'God,' they said, 'is on their side. Our game is up.' And maybe Rahab, seeing the corruption of Canaan, and hearing of the discipline that obtained in the Hebrew camp, sensed where final victory lay. And so she opted for the Hebrews, in other words, she chose the people of God, and did so by protecting their spies, on the strength of which she pleaded for her safety and her family's safety on the day when the assault of the city was mounted.

'Choose this day whom ye will serve,' cried Joshua to his own people in another passage recorded in the book that bears his name (24.15). Rahab for motives that were undoubtedly mixed, and were undoubtedly self-centred, chose to place her safety (her salvation) in the hands of the God of Israel. Yes, she was concerned about herself, but do not overlook the point that she was concerned for her whole family. Rahab was neither the first nor the last prostitute to work for her dependents. And do not overlook the desperate nature of her circumstances. Life and death, sustenance or starvation, liberty and slavery stared this woman in the face. A woman does not normally indulge, nor were these days for indulging, in philosophical speculation. You acted or you died, and God knows what motives lay mixed up in your decision.

But this is the point. God does know, God reads the human heart. God recognises that spark of faith amid the smouldering embers of fear and frustration which then become human urges towards self-preservation. Rahab, in all the coarseness of her sordid situation, believed sufficiently in the real God to act according to the meagre possibilities open to her. That is enough. It is enough in God's eyes to be 'counted for righteousness'. This woman was justified by faith, justified because in the sink of her surroundings she looked out and away towards the God of right living. Is it possible to pare down the good news of God's attitude to people further than this? This story of Rahab constitutes no approval of prostitution. It does not pass even a tiny carte blanche to the pornographers. What it does is to proclaim that however far down the scale of respectability we may have dropped, and however mixed may be our motives, if we want the righteous God, he will own us and we are counted as among his people, saved by choosing to belong, saved by faith.

Was Rahab a good woman? The answer is, no. Did she become a good woman? Well, her name is listed in the ancestry of Jesus recorded in St Matthew chapter one; and the eleventh chapter of the Epistle to the Hebrews (v. 31), sometimes called the Westminster Abbey of the Heroes of Faith, gives her a verse all to herself. So this is what the story of Rahab cries out to all of us—it does not signify in the eyes of God where we start in the pilgrimage of life, what signifies is the direction in which our faces are turned. It is what in our heart of hearts we really want to be that qualifies us, and not what we somehow manage to achieve.

11   THE GOSPEL ACCORDING TO RUTH

1 *A woman's book*

There is no love like a woman's love. It is different from the love of a man, even the love of a man for a woman, and I am not sure women always understand how different. But a woman's love stands by itself.

Chateaubriand in his book, *'Memoirs'* writes, 'She received me with that affection which only a sister can show. I felt safe and protected when I was enfolded in her arms; her ribbons, her lace and her bouquet of roses. Nothing can take the place of a woman's loyalty, delicacy and devotion; a man is forgotten by his brother and friends, and misjudged by his companions, but never by his mother, sister or his wife. When Harold was killed at the Battle of Hastings, his men could not recognise him among all the dead; they had to seek the help of a girl he loved. She came, and the unfortunate prince was found by Edith the Swannecked . . . '

Love is a woman's world. She moves in it naturally, and with a certain grace denied to men. You don't have to teach her about it, she comes to the knowledge intuitively. Men think hers a small world. Perhaps it is in one sense. Oscar Wilde, in his comedy, *An Ideal Husband* makes Lord Goring open Lady Chiltern's eyes about the breadth of man's world compared with women's world, and she was all the better for the understanding he imparted, but men who play big parts on the world stage of events in government, economics, science and defence, make a big mistake if they smile with a kind of superiority over women's world. It is important, most important, and to show how important, the Bible gives one whole book to the story of a woman's love.

Not everyone knows this. There is of course a woman's page in most newspapers, even those read by 'top people'. Few know that the Bible has a woman's book!

This book is placed squarely in the midst of historical works, works about guerrilla warfare, and the establishment of monarchical government. What more male pre-occupations than warfare and the law? But in between there is inserted a small book about a woman, indeed, it pays scarcely any attention to a man, except as may be necessary for a background, a little book of only four chapters and eighty-five verses, all about a woman's love crying aloud its insistent message that her domestic world must not be underrated. God never underrates it.

The book begins with a problem. Love so often is couched in problems. A small family uprooted by economic necessity tries to begin again in a new country. Father, mother and two sons. But the father dies just when the boys are taking notice of the local girls. How the father would have discouraged this! And if the truth were known, how disappointed was the mother! She would have liked her two boys to marry into two of the best families back at home. But what could you expect? For all they knew they must live for ever in the land of their adoption. Pity it was Moab, of course. The Moabites were bitter enemies of the Hebrews. Moses said no descendents of the Moabites could ever inherit in the land of Israel. And here were these two good-looking boys of Naomi, fit for any patrician daughter of some Jewish family, paying visits to Moab girls. What could she do?

Then the day broke when they announced impending marriage to these girls. So Naomi feared the prospect of Moabitesses in her closest family circle. That was her problem. Kings might have their problems, and army captains theirs. Naomi's problem was a problem of love, a domestic problem, the problem of a woman's world. Are you going to say it is unimportant? No woman would say so. Nor in fact does the Bible.

At least Naomi decided. Not, I guess, by rational consideration, but the heart has its reasons. She agreed to the marriage. So there were added to the family two swarthy looking girls, dark eyes, black hair, and withal such very foreign names, Orpah and Ruth.

Perhaps Naomi reasoned that anyway, the women would be her son's companions. They need not be her own. You need not 'hob-nob' much with your in-laws. But suddenly the picture changed. As if it were not tragic enough to lose possessions, homeland and husband, now her two sons died. What was there left close to her? Only two girls with foreign names, foreign faces, and doubtless a very marked foreign accent! Two women and their mother-in-law. A woman and two daughters-in-law. How would love survive in that relationship? We know what most would guess.

Then maybe Naomi saw the way of her escape. News was brought of improved conditions back at home. This would be the time to make a break. She would pack her things. She would cross the frontier. She would bid farewell to those Moabitish women. Not that she would find it easy now. Strange to say, she had grown attracted to these two strangers. Their united passage through bereavement had bound them all together. Better, however, a few tears now than years of uneasy, if not strained relationship. Yes, she would return at once to Bethlehem-judah.

3 *The unexpected*

But the unexpected happened. One daughter-in-law would not stay in Moab. She insisted on accompanying Naomi. Her words come ringing down the ages, 'Intreat me not to leave thee, or to return from following after thee: for whither thou goest, I will go; and where thou lodgest, I will lodge; thy people shall be my people, and thy God my God; Where thou diest, will I die, and there will I be buried: the Lord do so to me, and more also, if ought but death part thee and me.' This was Ruth.

And this is love. Woman's love. Love for a mother-in-law, an unexpected love, so some would say. But it brought her to Bethlehem, and in bringing her to Bethlehem, it brought her into Hebrew history. Ruth no longer is a foreign name. We have forgotten, if we ever knew, that it is Moabite. Ruth is now with the illustrious names of Israel's history. Abraham, Isaac, Jacob, Moses, Joshua, Ruth . . . . Not because she was unusually intelligent. Such did exist in Israel. Not that she was outstandingly beautiful. Such women are spoken of within the sacred records. Ruth has taken her place among the great because she was true to what lies at the heart of every woman's world—love. In Ruth we see it at its best, unobtrusive, unassuming and completely unaggressive.

But there is more to it than this. If we could enter into a picture gallery containing portraits of the complete ancestry of Jesus, and could scan the Jewish features of them all, we would ask as there was pointed out a woman's face, 'But who is that, the woman with the foreign eyes, the dark skin and the peculiar style of hair? Why is she there?' The answer is, her name is Ruth. For after she had crossed the frontier to settle down with Naomi in Judah, she eventually married Boaz. They had a child called Obed, and Obed was the father of one called Jesse, and Jesse was the father of David, of whose lineage Jesus was born. And born where? In the same village where Ruth settled, Bethlehem in the land of Judah.

4 The gospel

So now there is a gospel according to Ruth. Wherever love reigns, God recognises it. In a woman's world, in a woman's heart, in a foreign woman's heart, whose marriage constituted a problem. Virtue is virtue wherever it is found. In a Samaritan on the Jericho road, rescuing a traveller. In a Vietcong in the jungle showing mercy to a wounded Yank. In a back street with a Neopolitan girl comforting a homeless urchin. Did the post-exilic particularists of Israel find this gospel hard to accept when they found the book of Ruth in circulation in their midst? Do we find it unacceptable today? Race relations is one of our problems. But virtue is virtue wherever it is found, and across whatever frontiers. And love is a virtue, woman's love, sacrificial, unassuming, unobtrusive love. God claimed it for his own by incorporating Ruth into the family tree of Christ. Do not underrate woman's world. Do not under-estimate virtue in an unexpected place. Do not be unexpectant of surprises in experience. Above all, remember love is the mainspring of the telling acts in life. 'God so loved the world, that he gave . . .' God's love. Our love in response. That is where the gate of heaven stands. Such is our proclamation. Such is our gospel, the gospel growing out of the woman's book in the Old Testament, the slender book of Ruth.

12 MOTHER—SON—GRANDSONS

Not long ago there lay on the desk of one of the leaders of British life a letter advising what action should be taken over one of the trouble spots in the Middle East. It was a balanced and well-informed letter, so much so that it did not appear incongruous lying there waiting for a responsible answer. Nor were there grounds for incongruity. Nevertheless the background, unknown to the recipient, was that the writer happened to be the daughter of a London policeman, who, with his wife, made it a priority that their two children should receive the benefit of a God-fearing home and every educational advantage that lay within their power to provide. No wonder the children advanced to positions of leadership.

The Old Testament is a book about nations and kings, but it does not fail to trace the great movements of history which it describes back to people, back to homes, and back to parents. The Old Testament remembers what we too often forget, that heredity and home environment are the formative factors in the lives of people, and through people in the life of the nation.

1 *Mother*

Perhaps this is most elaborately set out in the case of Samuel. Samuel ushered in one of the most brilliant periods of Hebrew history. With him there took place the founding of the monarchy and the formation of schools of prophets, and nothing could have been more fundamental to subsequent Hebrew life than the contribution of kings and prophets and their interplay. But behind all this lay a praying woman, a woman who felt deprived being childless in her marriage, if not humiliated. Eschewing bitterness, however, she continued to pray, and not only to pray, but to hear with a believing heart the promise that her prayer would be answered; and as if that were insufficient, to vow that this child would be dedicated to the Lord for his whole life. It sounds commonplace. But this dedication involved separation from her child, it meant reassuming a life of virtual childlessness, the cessation of a boy's laughter in the home, and the loss of her early morning kiss. There was self-sacrifice where a woman feels it most, not in the realm of power, time or money, but in the kingdom of the heart, of life and of love. But she gave, and her husband perceiving the cost added his 'yes' to the sacrifice. What parents they were! What a faith was theirs consisting not simply in asking and receiving, but in renunciation and giving.

Such was the context of the early life of Samuel, the first great man in Israel since the death of Moses, whose mother also was a woman of faith and a woman of resource. Indeed, in the cases of these first two great leaders it is their mothers and not their fathers that stand out in the records. And for fear lest it be assumed that piety alone was the characteristic of Samuel's mother, let it be noted that the compiler of the book of Samuel thought fit to attach to her name a poetic piece which deserves to stand for its literary excellence beside any of the Psalms of David, and is so obviously the source of the inspiration of Mary's song in the New Testament that it has carried the title 'the Magnificat of the Old Testament'. According to the Bible the key to Samuel's greatness will not be found if this woman, his mother, is overlooked.

Women are responsible for quality in a nation. If women become degraded then the nation's progress towards disintegration will be rapid. If women are ill-educated, the result will be a coarsening on the part of the public as a whole. The tendency is always for men to use women. At the lowest level to use them as means for the gratification of their sexual impulses. Could this come out more strongly than in the recent television series on the *Story of the Abolition of Slavery*, when a half-drunken white plantation owner in the West Indies descended after dinner to the cellar to bed down with a black slave girl, commanding first as he uncovered her nakedness, 'Turn out the light, so that I do not see your ugly black face.' But women have been used in other ways, as cheap labour, slaves in the home, slaves on the factory floor, slaves to operate the new electronic calculators. But the most alarming feature of all is the extent to which women's bodies are being exploited for financial gain. Big money is being made in this field. All of which is a long way from the view the Bible takes of women, namely, a help meet for man, with spiritual gifts and intellectual accomplishments in her own right, one of the springs of a nation's greatness it earths up to its detriment.

2 Mother and son

And now we turn to look at the relationships of mother and son. There is no love like that of a mother for her child. This love stands in a category by itself. For one reason it is more perceptive than that of a man for his wife, or even of a wife for her husband. It oberves details. It watches for trends in character. It marks similarities and differences from other members of the family. There is no interest like that of a mother, even for her grown-up son. Of course it can be counter-productive. This happens when a child is over-mothered. But Samuel did not run this risk. He was separated from his mother's presence, in adolescence, if not childhood, but her love and her interest did not wane. Every year she visited him in Shiloh taking a present of a little cloak. A child has no mother if she does not with her love and with her interest, also give presents, which presents indeed, become sacraments of that love and interest.

The Lutheran Bible picks up a point in this scene of Samuel as a boy ministering in the temple at Shiloh, which the English versions miss. At chapter 2.18, it reads, 'But Samuel was a servant before the Lord.' This was the secret of Samuel's uniqueness. As his mother gave, so did he. Samuel was not simply a priest. God has had many priests, but only a few servants. There are good priests who fulfil their ministries faithfully and there are bad priests who disgrace their calling by their laziness. A servant of God, however, is more than a good priest. He is one who places his entire life in God's hands. This is what Samuel's mother did. Her child was her life, but she gave it to God. This also Samuel did. Everything about himself he placed at God's disposal, and it constituted his strength.

One other picture sets Samuel in the following of his mother. There came a day when the Hebrews were hard pressed by the Philistines. Annihilation stared them in the face so they cried out to Samuel, 'Do not cease to pray for us to the Lord our God to save us from the power of the Philistines.' (I Samuel 7.8) Do not cease to pray! Apparently the people recognised his secret. Had he not already 'summoned all Israel to an assembly at Mizpah, so that he might intercede with the Lord for them'? And are we not told in almost the last report of him that at his home in Ramah he built an altar unto the Lord? (Chapter 7.17) Prayer was the secret of his own life. Like mother, like son. It could almost be said Samuel was conceived by prayer. He was throughout life a servant of the Lord. No minister, no ministry, no Church, can be the Lord's servant unless it gives and unless it prays.

3 Grandsons

But what happened to Samuel's home? To pinpoint the enquiry—Whom had Samuel married? We are not told. But how came it that Samuel's sons did not follow in their father's footsteps? How was it that they did not become servants of the Lord, but sought instead what they could gain and not what they could give? As judges in the land they took bribes and perverted the course of justice. How was this? Was Samuel so occupied as virtually the sole leader in the land—priest, prophet and judge—that he gave no time to his home? Preoccupation with work, good work, work on behalf of others, even God's work, has caused men to neglect their homes since Samuel's day. Was it a case of too much power, too much money corrupting? The history books are sprinkled with the accounts of children born with silver spoons in their mouths who have not made good. A father's shoulders would seem to be the most advantageous place from which to begin the march through life, but so often leaders derive from those who have been forced to struggle to their own feet. We protest that a family ought to be able to leave its wealth to its successors, but when it comes to character, those same successors seem only infrequently to benefit. Greatness, apparently, is not inherited automatically, nor are material advantages its guarantors. Better straightened circumstances with a God-fearing home than riches without a mother's prayers, discipline and love.

So Samuel passes off the scene. A man from a good home who rose to leadership and power, but whose sons did not follow in his steps. Grandmother, son, grandsons. Where are we in these three tiers? Where would we opt to be? Everything in the God-man relationship depends in the end on what we really want. There are many things, many stations in life we cannot choose, but one thing we can, we can choose to be men and women of prayer, and who knows what benefits may accrue? This is the lesson of Samuel's story.

13   WAITING FOR GOD

2 Kings 6.33 *'Why should I wait for the Lord any longer?'*

Three hundred years ago, or thereabouts, King William III set out from Kensington Palace to make the journey to Holland. He was a Dutchman who hoped that his new position as King of England could be used to strengthen Holland against its old enemy, France. And so he frequently returned to Holland. But this time the journey was particularly difficult. The storms in the Thames Estuary and North Sea would not subside. Of course he could have risked them but it would have been madness. So he turned aside with Mary, his Queen, to stay with Tillotson, then Dean of Canterbury, waiting in their house for the storms to cease.

There are some situations in life where the wisest course of action is not to act, but to wait. This is a hard lesson and the men of impulse find it almost impossibly hard. Such, for instance, was Napoleon; indeed, it was his impatience which in the end brought him down. He could not wait for the favourable time. He could not wait for reinforcements. So convinced was he of his own genius that he reckoned he could hack a way through any circumstances. This was his mistake. Life is not so arranged that any man can act in this way. All have to learn in some form the lesson of waiting.

1 *A people's plight*

The story of Jehoram King of Israel (812–860 BC) brings to our attention the wisdom at times of waiting. It belongs to the years when Benhadad, King of Syria, was besieging Israel's capital city, Samaria. It was a shattering time, how shattering the writer of 2 Kings 6 lets us see. 'The city was near starvation and they besieged it so closely that a donkey's head was sold for eighty shekels of silver and a quarter of a kab of locust-beans for five shekels.' So in the scarcity food prices rocketed. Indeed, to such desperate plights were the citizens reduced that the King, walking on the wall encountered two women quarrelling because each had agreed to kill and share her child for food; but when the one did it, the other refused. This was too much for King Jehoram. He swore that he would take it out of Elisha the prophet (which really meant taking it out of God), for allowing such miseries to befall them. He would kill Elisha.

And now the scene shifts and we see Elisha the prophet sitting in his house in the city with the elders; and suddenly and urgently bidding that the door be reinforced against the king's messenger because the king himself would be behind him bent on murder. But the order was insufficiently swift, for in a moment the king was there inside the house shaking (we may suppose) with anger. 'Look at our plight,' he shouted. 'This is the Lord's doing. Why should I wait for the Lord any longer?' But no sword was drawn. Instead Elisha prophesied—'Hear the word of the Lord. Tomorrow about this time shall a measure of fine flour be sold for a shekel, and two measures of barley for a shekel, in the gate of Samaria.' Within twenty-four hours food will be plentiful and cheap. And if we possess imagination we can see pity written across the face of the king's officer that a prophet should be reduced to such ridiculous utterance. 'Behold', he said, 'if the Lord should make windows in heaven might this thing be.' But swiftly the retort came back from Elisha, 'You will see it with your eyes but you will not taste thereof.'

2 A people's leaders

'Why should I wait for the Lord any longer?' Jehoram was not a bad king, indeed, considering that he was the son of Ahab he was a remarkably good king. When those two quarrelling women saw him rend his clothes aghast at the desperate plight to which the common people were reduced, they noticed how he was wearing a hair shirt next to his skin—so closely did he identify himself with the misery of his subjects. We must not be hard on Jehoram. In any case who is there of us who hasn't at some time cried out against God and felt mad about his Church, because our world has fallen, and is constantly falling, into such inhuman misery as bloodthirsty war. Why doesn't God do something, something for me? Perhaps he can't! Perhaps he won't! Either way, 'Why should I wait for the Lord any longer?'

And now we turn to look at Elisha. Elisha was a prophet. Elisha's business, therefore (ought we to say his sole business?), was to declare the word of the Lord. When Jehoram cried out, 'Why should I wait for the Lord?' Elisha answered, 'Hear the word of the Lord.' Perhaps the Church constantly needs to be reminded that its prime task is to declare the word of the Lord. From time to time there arises a tendency for the Church to see itself as primarily a relief organisation. But to defend the people and to care for the people is the primary task of the State. The Church must of course show the State its duty and set it an example, but no more. Elisha was God's minister, but King Jehoram was also God's minister, each with different spheres of responsibility. The king must not oust the prophet and the prophet must not try to oust the king. It is for the prophet, it is for the Church to declare what God has done, is doing, and will do tomorrow, and if it fails it has failed in its prime responsibility.

And God's action came swiftly. The very next day the

Syrian armies dispersed. What is more, they dispersed for nothing more substantial than reported rumblings of Egyptian war machines (just as if Israel would have hired such against them!) So God overthrew steel with a puff of rumour, crying aloud that he is neither dead, asleep nor purposeless. On the contrary, God is the sovereign Lord of Kings, even of King Demos who can be a tyrant. All kings indeed lie in the hollow of God's hand. No surprise therefore need attach to this story of fantastic deliverance, fantastic because swift, complete and in a fashion, ridiculous. Invaders dispersing because of a noise! But fantastic too because the heralds of the deliverance were four lepers, who, wandering as they must, outside the city walls discovered the Syrian tents deserted and cried, 'This is a day of good tidings and we hold our peace.' But fantastic even more because when the astonishing news entered into the ears of the starving city dwellers they rushed the city gate to get at the food, trampling to death in their crowded madness the king's officer who had retorted to Elisha, 'If the Lord should make windows in heaven, might this thing be.'

3 *A proper attitude*

What is the lesson of this story? It is to wait upon God for his salvation. The French have a saying, *Tout vient à point à qui sait attendre*. 'Everything comes to him who knows how to wait for it' Does it? There is no certainty; but to this the Bible bears testimony, that everything good comes to him who knows how to wait upon God for it. Or in the words of Psalm 37, 'Rest in the Lord, and wait patiently for him' or Psalm 62, 'My soul truly waiteth still upon God: for of him cometh my salvation.' But man does not readily wait for God's salvation. Over and over again in the Bible pictures are supplied of men's reluctance to wait for God. King Saul offering the sacrifice and sinning because he could not wait for the prophet Samuel to fulfil his proper office. The steward in our Lord's parable complaining, 'My Lord delayeth his coming' and proceeding to ill-treat his fellow servants. And the general cry of impatient men echoing from the second epistle of St Peter, 'Where is the promise of his coming? From the first day that the fathers fell asleep all things continue as they were from the beginning of creation.' But the message of the Bible does not waver—'The Lord is a God of judgement, blessed are all they that wait for him.'

What does this mean for us in practice? It means that we must look for God's saving acts on behalf of men for their deliverance, damaging though this is to human pride. Individuals cannot, society cannot, save itself. Man needs God's intervention for his own safety.

Secondly, we must allow for God's judgements to operate among the world's injustices, or as St Paul expressed it, " 'Vengeance is mine, I will repay', saith the Lord."

Thirdly, we should see tomorrow's uncertainties through the eyes of faith in a God who has his own methods of deliverance, some of them contrary to our human calculations. We can never forecast what God will do for the benefit of people, which is why we should 'rest in the Lord and wait patiently for him.'

14 A NATION'S DEFENCES

2 Kings 13.4 (NEB) *'My father! My father, the chariots and the horsemen of Israel!'*

We begin with a wholly imaginary scene. It is Lambeth Palace, the London residence of the Archbishops of Canterbury since 1197. In one of the rooms the Archbishop's long life of sacrificial labour on behalf of the Church and nation is drawing to its close. That labour throughout the years has not been made easier by the sovereign across the river, taking no stand whatsoever for ideals, values or morals, either in his own life or in that of the nation at large. But now the Archbishop is dying, and to everyone's surprise, the royal car slips swiftly over Lambeth Bridge to enter the Palace through Morton's gateway. It is the sovereign himself paying his last respects to the Archbishop he has consistently ignored. And as if the visit itself were not sufficiently astonishing, on meeting the nation's spiritual leader in his last hours, the king declares with all the sincerity of which he is capable, 'You have done more to protect this nation than all the armed forces of the crown put together.'

This scene is wholly imaginary, but the Bible brings our attention to a piece of history which is similar. In 2 Kings 13.14, King Jehoash, listed in scripture as one of the kings of Israel who 'did what was wrong in the eyes of the Lord', heard that Elisha had fallen ill and lay on his death bed. This, as it happened, was to be the last day in Elisha's long life devoted to demonstrating the reality and power of God in an era of unbelief. And now the king himself stood by the prophet's bedside. What could it have been that made him come? Did he suddenly sense, for all his neglect of the God of Israel, that ultimately the nation's strength lay in him? Did remorse suddenly enter this royal heart that he had so consistently rejected this holy man of God? Who can tell? All we know is that suddenly he burst into tears crying, 'My father! My father, the chariots and the horsemen of Israel!' These were the words Elisha himself had uttered, when, as a young man, he had watched his master Elijah carried up in a whirlwind to heaven. 'My father! My father, the chariots and the horsemen of Israel!', meaning surely that Elijah and Elisha, for all the neglect, opposition and downright persecution these men of God had suffered at the hands of the occupants of the thrones of their day, had done more by their spiritual leadership for the protection of the nation than all the chariots and horsemen of Israel put together, yes, and their subtle political machinations, too.

Did the light suddenly break into King Jehoash's heart? We shall never know, any more than we shall ever be able to plumb the mystery of that tyrant, if not monster, King Henry VIII dying and calling for Archbishop Cranmer, and finding no peace till Cranmer took the king's hand in his. And then he enquired, 'Are you trusting in Christ?' and the king squeezed the Archbishop's hand for his affirmative reply, and so he died, king and Archbishop hand in hand. . . .

'My father! My father, the chariots and the horsemen of Israel!'

1 National strength

But can we accept this? Is not this statement sentimental, unrealistic and emotional? Must we not rate it as the unreliable outburst of a man thrown off his balance by the strain of a moving scene? All of us have moments when we experience sentiments such as these. That morning when Churchill's draped coffin lay under the dome of St Paul's and up in the whispering gallery against a blank wall a trumpeter played the Last Post, to be followed by a second trumpeter standing before the glass of an unstained window playing the Reveille! Was this not a moment of sudden transportation to another plane of living? But the worshippers had to leave the Cathedral to re-establish with the bustle out on Ludgate Hill. Is not Ludgate Hill the real world and that moment in St Paul's a fancy world? King Jehoash! Sir, I expect you came down to earth when you quitted Elisha's death-chamber? Or did you not, because you could not eject from your mind what Elisha made you do before you left, which is why the story has remained crystallised to this day in 2 Kings 13.14–19. Could it be that these fleeting moments contain windows looking at reality, or must we write them off as futile unreality?

What is the source of a nation's strength? We have heard the answer in our day till we are almost wearied with the hearing—economic growth, and yet more economic growth! What is the source of a nation's strength? Technological expertise, and yet more technological expertise! What is the source of a nation's strength? Democratic government! The voice of the people! Worker participation! We hear it till we are aware that we are scarcely listening. And welfare, we calculate, will disinfect the breeding grounds of social discontent and keep the revolutionaries at bay. Meanwhile, the nuclear deterrent stands poised, this is the ultimate national safeguard, if not the conventional forces.

'My father! My father, the chariots and the horsemen of Israel!' Are these words sentimental nonsense? The question is not irrelevant in the western world today when we note the build-up of those national defences represented by economic growth, technology, democratic participation, welfare and the bomb, and at the same time, note the slow breakdown in the western world of a life that is satisfying. Futility indeed, uncertainty and pointlessness, appear to be gaining ground. Where ultimately is a nation's security? What are its real defences? Is it not to this question that 2 Kings 13 addresses its reply? 'My father! My father, the chariots and the horsemen of Israel!'

2 Men of God

Men of God is what the scripture answers. Men of the stature of Elijah and Elisha. Men with the faith of Elijah and Elisha, men who witness to that faith against odds, men who demonstrate their faith by action, by protest, by conflict and by beneficial acts of mercy to the unfortunate. Men of God in a nation are a nation's defences. And we cringe before this answer! A philosophy sprinkled with the abstract nouns, 'values', 'morals' and 'insight' we might have suffered—a nation's ultimate strength is in its sense of moral values! But 2 Kings is offensively concrete, personal and practical. When there are leaders in a nation who actively believe in the Word of God (this is the characteristic of a prophet), then there is a source of strength, and an ultimate defence.

Why? Because a man of God is both a sign and an agent.

A man of God is a sign. He is a sign that God exists. He is a sign that God is active. God apparently calls men, unless, of course, we are prepared to write off the men of God as deluded fanatics, or men in the 'religion business' for what they can get out of it! But were Elijah and Elisha subnormal? Was Isaiah a crank? And Jeremiah a nincompoop? Was Jesus of Nazareth a time server? Then how have the words of these men been preserved to this day, still teasing the intelligences and consciences of even the educated in so far as they are prepared to listen? And what did Elisha and

Elijah profit by the 'religion business'? What did Isaiah and Jeremiah gain? What did Jesus receive? Golgotha will tell us! This is the point, wherever there exist men of God whose quality of life is outstanding and whose profit by worldly standards is meagre, if not non-existent, there you have the signs that God not only exists, but that he calls men into his distinctive service.

Secondly, a man of God is an agent of God, that is to say, God works through him. Apart from the story of Jesus in the gospels there is nowhere in the Bible bearing stronger testimony to this than the second book of Kings with its account of Elisha. Let it be said that some of these miracle stories in the Elisha saga are legendary, still the narrative cries aloud its message that not only is the man of God a sign that God exists, but that God is active through him on behalf of his people, yes, even in a period such as that of the reign of Jehoash when its people as a whole paid scant attention to the faith of its forefathers.

3 The Church of God

Is there not here a strong reminder concerning the Church of God in the nation? In so far as the Church is evidently a congregation of men of God, it is both a sign of God's existence, and an agent of his purpose. But it must be a Church of quality, a Church of intelligence and goodness, a Church which bears the marks of leadership; and it must also be a Church that is seen not to profit by its profession.

Perhaps the economic stringency of the times is presenting the Church today with a new opportunity. Only men of deep conviction will stay with the Church in the latter half of the twentieth century. Soon the Church's ministers will be at the end of the line as far as monetary rewards are concerned.

There is a story of a visitor arriving at a stately home as a guest for the night. The chauffeur was surprised when he met him at the station, for there was only a rucksack to carry by way of luggage and a raincoat. And when this humble luggage was carried to the spare bedroom, it looked odd against the Jacobean furniture. But at dinner the black-cassocked figure relished the claret equally with his host, and was a match in conversation on eighteenth-century literature, not least first editions. Here clearly was a man of God who had nothing and yet possessed all things, a picture, perhaps, of what the Church ought, and may come, to be.

'My father! My father, the chariots and the horsemen of Israel!' A nation is strong when it possesses men of God. A nation is strong when it counts among its members a true Church of God, that is a Church of spiritual stature and a Church indifferent to its comfort.

There came a day in the life of the Hebrew people when outside their capital city, of which they were justly proud, there sat a man on a donkey surrounded by ecstatic crowds. His eyes, which had so frequently opened with wonder at Jerusalem's magnificence, clouded over and filled with tears. True on that day the pilgrim crowds were acclaiming him. They saw in him their saviour, their protector, their bulwark and their strength. 'My father! My father, the chariots and the horsemen of Israel!' But the recognition would be short lived. They would crucify their man of God within the week. Therefore he wept over his city. It did not know 'the things which belonged to its peace.' Consistently it had killed the prophets and stoned them which had been sent into it.

What will Britain do with its Church today? What will the Church do with itself? Will it be a prophet in and for the state? Only then can any one exclaim in its presence, 'My father! My father, the chariots and the horsemen of Israel!'

15   THE UNENDING GOSPEL

2 Kings 17.20 ' . . . *So the Lord rejected the whole race of Israel'*

It was an impressive block of flats occupying one of the most expensive sites in London. And now the demolition squad was at work on it. Not because it was unsafe or substandard, but because if it were rebuilt with flats having lower ceilings, more could be accommodated and the income from rents correspondingly increased. A huge pile of broken bricks and plaster dominated what was once the spacious forecourt. A fierce crackling fire was consuming the mahogany woodwork that once graced those West End residences. And there high up on almost the last remaining wall stood a man with a pick-axe watched by a little gathering of spectators on the pavement below. Perhaps it was the yellow patterned wallpaper that caught their eye, and the simple set of bookshelves on the wall. It could have been a child's bedroom, full of memories. But the pick-axe brought it down in a moment to add to the giant pile of rubble below. So without ceremony or dignity that impressive block of flats came to its end, and with it the stories of many human dramas that had been lived out within its walls, stories of love, tragedy, expensive sordidness, and astonishing goodness. Soon there would be nothing left but the memory of what had happened there from the Edwardian era, two world wars and the 1960s. The site was flattened and the mind flattened at the thought of it.

1 *History*

In 2 Kings chapter 17, we read of a similar demolition, not of a building, but of a kingdom, the Northern Kingdom of Israel. It happened in 722 B.C., the outcome of the invasion of the land by Assyria's deadly war machine. There are no frills in this section of the Biblical narrative, no miracles, no chariots of fire, no angels, nor even the report of such as at Mons in 1914. Nothing here strains the credulity. The same glasses as are worn to read *The Times* will suffice for this account. In bold, terse, almost monotonous terms it tells of the toppling of what had been a magnificent kingdom, graced by men like Elijah and Elisha, Amos, Hosea, and a host of others. Now its long day is at its end, all we see is one last man standing before he too crashes, a political figure, an upstart with blood on his hands, for he gained the throne by the murder of his predecessor, as in fact that predecessor had done himself. But this man, King Hoshea, does not stand for long. Shalmaneser, the King of Assyria swings his mighty axe, and down he comes, toppling down, and all the kingdom with him.

2 *Analysis*

What brought about the downfall of the kingdom of Israel? This question could initiate an historical enquiry, and as such would have its proper place, but the Old Testament is not primarily a set of history lessons, it is preaching. It aims at proclaiming the message that godliness constitutes a nation's security, and rebellion against God precedes calamity. The compiler of the second book of Kings provides meagre details of the immediate causes of King Hoshea's downfall beyond informing us that he obtained the throne by murdering its occupant, and withheld paying tribute to Assyria, seeking meanwhile a secret understanding with Egypt. Regicide and political intrigue are incriminating enough, even so the account assures us that Hoshea was not as evil as his predecessors. So caution is issued not to lay the blame for Israel's collapse at one man's door—Hoshea—but to lay it at the door of the nation which had produced an Hoshea and many others worse before him. All the ills, those within Israel, and those that befell Israel, stem from the rebellion against the house of David when Jeroboam, son of Nebat was proclaimed a rival King. Rebellion against God, the Maker of Israel, is placarded in this scripture as the root cause of the nation's downfall, and it works itself out in three main directions, false (that is, idolatrous) worship, contravention of the established law and order, and political intrigue, the final two proceeding from the first. 'So', says verse 20 of this seventeenth chapter, 'the Lord rejected the whole race of Israel . . . .'

3 *The Message*

Is this message applicable to us? Can it be applied at all to any modern state? Is there a word here for Britain in our day?

At first sight the answer is doubtful. Modern states do not

recognise their existence as stemming from any act, or series of acts, of God in the historical past. Israel was intended to be a theocracy. Modern states purport to be democracies. There exists, therefore, no binding element in faith and no binding element in ethical practice (except what is residual from the past when the Church enjoyed a certain dominance), to make a national rebellion as envisaged by the second book of Kings possible. When a society is both secular and pluralist it appears that the preaching of this scripture cannot be heard, it is in-applicable to our situation.

Before, however, we close the book and deafen our ears to the preachers, we ought to ask another question. Does a moral law operate in community living at all? Does it matter if dishonesty, grasping, greed and envy infiltrate a whole society? That is to say, is there any experienced or foreseeable consequence? By the 1970s in Britain these questions were being thrust from every quarter, not as classroom queries, but as anxious whispers from hard-headed business men conscious of catastrophe as a coming possibility. There is little trust any more, little trust of politicians, little trust of economists, little trust of the financial wizards, little trust on the part of employers, little trust on the part of employees. Few people believe in anything. Fewer still believe in anyone. The urgent question then erects its ugly head—in such a state can a community cohere?—And if it cannot cohere, can it survive? The answer of the Old Testament is 'No'. According to the prophets, significantly Amos, moral laws operated even outside Israel and their deliberate contravention spells destruction.

4 *The Response*

So what shall we do? If dishonesty flows from false worship as the Old Testament avers, shall we enforce religion? The question only needs to be framed to be rejected. Some of the bloodiest pages in our history books tell the story of these attempts. *Cuius regio eius religio* (one state, one religion) does not work. But what about a moral reform for the nation's good backed by law? The prophet Jeremiah saw the attempt in Israel and tasted disillusionment. The only way is preaching. Goodness cannot be commanded, it can only be commended. And it is commended not only by words but by deeds, not only by theories but by people, people who are the embodiment of what they believe, people in whose hearts secretly, the laws of God are written. This is the new preaching of the Old Testament, the new preaching on the lips of Jeremiah, who witnessed the failure of the law to remake his rebellious compatriots. But everything in the last resort depends on a theology. If a people turn back, will God forgive and remake? What does the moral law declare?—Nothing! What do the history books offer? Yes, even the historical narrative in 2 Kings chapter 17? Nothing beyond the verdict—'. . . So the Lord rejected the whole race of Israel and punished them and gave them over to plunderers and finally flung them out of his sight.' But what does God say? God, through the words of his prophets, yes, in the Old Testament itself . . . 'Return unto me and I will return unto you.' So the process of remaking can be initiated through response to the word of the preaching, the word of promise, the word of forgiveness, leading to the creation of a new and better life. This is the new preaching from the Old Testament, pointing its finger to the everlasting gospel, so that St Paul could write even in the face of 2 Kings 17.20, 'God has not rejected the people which he acknowledged of old as his own. . . . O depth of wealth, wisdom, and knowledge in God! How unsearchable his judgements, how untraceable his ways!' Romans 11.2,33 (NEB)

16   SILENT BUT STRONG

2 Kings 18.36 *'The people were silent and answered not a word.'*

This scripture draws our attention to a man making a speech, and what he has to say bears a remarkable similarity to what the world is at the present time saying to the Church, and in some measure always has said. This speech-maker is an Assyrian, a chief officer, technically called Rabshakeh; and as he speaks there is lined up behind him the might of the Assyrian army terrible to behold. And this Rabshakeh stands facing the walls of Jerusalem, indeed, he is only a few yards distant and all along the walls are huddled the ordinary folk of Jerusalem, hungry, emaciated and diseased, broken, or all but broken by a seige of their city that has already lasted too long. And this Rabshakeh calls for the king to come out and surrender, but the king does not appear. Through the gate, however, there walk three men sent to meet Rabshakeh hoping perhaps to parley with him on behalf of the king. But Rabshakeh does not parley, instead he makes a speech and such a loud one that all the people on the walls can hear, which, of course, was his intention.

If the year had been A.D. 1976 instead of 701 B.C. the means of the speech would have been television or sound radio, but the purpose would have been the same—to cause as many people as possible to receive the message—and the content would have been the same (that is the surprising fact). The object of the exercise would be to encircle the Church, wearing it down by force of argument till it finally surrenders.

Where are you in this picture? Where am I? Where is every worshipping congregation? It is up on the walls afraid, listening to the disturbing words of this Rabshakeh, this chief officer of a hostile people.

1 *The taunt*

And what does he say to those he intends to crush? First, he says, 'All you possess is words. But if you seek influence you should calculate situations and intervene strategically with power. "Realpolitik" is the only effective approach. Why not have recourse to political action? Why not throw in your resources behind the "freedom movements" resorting to force to obtain the results you desire? What can talking effect? Remember, no values defend themselves.'

What else does this Rabshakeh say? He says in effect, 'You Church people are not all that faithful to the God you profess to trust, are you? You make great boast of your confidence in God's power to sustain, but where would you be without the Church Commissioners' money? Where would you be without these impressive buildings your fathers have left as your inheritance? Where would you be without the State connection which gives you precedence in the eyes of men? Why not strip yourselves of your possessions? Isn't this what your God wants you to do? And if you refuse, will he not punish you beyond repair?'

And we Church people lining the walls have knocking knees as we listen to this Rabshakeh making his subtle speech. There is truth in his propaganda which is why it is so devastating. We do not trust wholly in God. We do only live at peace when we can see how next year's balance sheet is going to look. And few relish the idea of disestablishment if it means disendowment!

So what shall we do? Surrender to this Rabshakeh? Stop our ears and refuse to listen? But the criticisms of the world ought to be taken seriously by the Church. On one point only should we pay scant attention. It is when the world (represented by this Rabshakeh) tries to tell us about God. It knows very little about God and even less about God's forgiveness. After all, how can it know?

2 The offer

We return to the story. Half way through Rabshakeh's speech the deputation of three appealed to him to speak, not in Hebrew but in Aramaic, so that the people on the walls could not understand and be disturbed in their minds. But they might as well have addressed the walls themselves for Rabshakeh spoke louder than ever in Hebrew so they could understand, and this is what he said.

'Don't let your king deceive you. He is keeping you down, but I, Rabshakeh, will set you free if you submit to me.'

This is an old trick but it succeeds too often to be despised.

Poor people, poor Church people, you are kept in order by your priests, pastors and preachers. They feed you on silly fables and antiquated legends when you could be set free to move in the healthy uplands of science and sociology. Why don't you shake off your repressive spiritual guides and enjoy the freedom which the world at once will grant you?

And there is truth in Rabshakeh's propaganda speech. Our priests and pastors are not all enlightened men or even holy men or happy men. Some are dull, drab and overbearing with no real understanding of the joy and liberty of the children of God—but it is an old trick to separate the people from their leaders. 'Divide the rule' is the classic phrase. And now in the 1970s the campaign is on to tear Christian people away from the organised Church. The contemporary Rabshakeh is pouring his sweet blandishments into our ears—Christ is splendid, the Church is feeble. To be a Christian is noble. To be a Churchman is stupid. Up with Jesus. Down with the priests. Believe Rabshakeh and then you will be free.

But the Rabshakeh is a liar. In this century we have seen what the self-professed liberators do. The Russians poured into Prague to set the inhabitants free from their terrible local masters, but how is Prague today? Is it free?

The odd fact about this Rabshakeh's speech in 2 Kings 18 is that it might have been said by some contemporary politicians bent on subduing the Church. 'Ask yourselves,' he says, "what has your religion done for you? Have not science, industry and psychology been responsible for all your benefits? And what has Christianity protected you from? From wars? From strikes? From inflation?' Rabshakeh does not use these words, of course, he says, 'Where are the gods of Hamath and Arpad, of Sepharvaim, Hena and Ivvah? Has any of them saved his land from the king of Assyria?'

And we wince, all of us, lined up on the wall of our Jerusalem—because this speech is clever. He knows the location of our wounds wherein to thrust his knife and when to turn it!

3 The silence

And what happened? What happened when this Rabshakeh had finished his speech? What reaction was there among those frightened people, hungry and emaciated, standing on Jerusalem's walls? And the answer is—there was no reaction. They kept silent and Rabshakeh went away—because their king had said, 'Answer him not a word.'

We ought to pay attention to what they did. When the world blares at the Church with its propaganda, some of it true, most of it false, the right course is to keep silence, the wrong course is to argue back. The Church will never beat the world in the game of political propaganda. What King Hezekiah did and what God did can be read in 2 Kings chapter 19. Suffice it to draw attention to the Hebrew proverb, 'There is a time to speak and a time to refrain from speaking'. And the time to refrain from speaking is when Rabshakeh issues half truths as weapons of offence. Remember Jesus in the court room at the end. 'The chief priests accused him of many things: but he answered nothing. And Pilate asked him again, saying 'Answerest thou nothing? Behold how many things they witness against thee.'' But Jesus yet answered nothing; so that Pilate marvelled.'

Silence before the accuser can be a sign of strength. It can also be a sign of trust in God's promise of protection, and a mark of obedience. It was this latter with the people on the walls accused by Rabshakeh. They were at least obedient to their king who told them to answer not a word. It was the command and the obedience which gave them what strength they had. We could at least show this steadfastness in times of trial, praying for the guidance of God when not to speak. And then we would be strong, strong in our silence, strong like our Master Jesus, sufficiently strong, perhaps, even to make Pilate, or Rabshakeh, or our modern accuser, marvel.

[I am indebted for the idea of this sermon to *The Politics of God and the Politics of Man* by Jacques Ellul (1972).]

15 THE SCRIBE

Ezra 7.28 *'So, knowing that the hand of the Lord my God was upon me, I took courage.'*

1 *Ezra the man*

Who was Ezra? Ezra was a scholar born in desolate conditions on the torrid plains of the Euphrates valley. He came of a Jewish priestly family and could trace his ancestry back to Aaron when he hadn't better things to do. He had never known anything else but exile. He had never lived in his own land of Judah, never felt the cooling winds on its rugged hills, never ministered at an altar, never seen any magnificent form of worship in the Jerusalem temple of his fathers. For him life was a drab affair of prison huts and drab routines.

But Ezra didn't go under. That is the first point to notice. In general look for your leaders among those whose upbringing was hard, men who know privation in youth but don't go under. Those are the men to watch.

Secondly, note that Ezra was a scholar. You can't have leaders destitute of book learning. And while the other priests of notable pedigree were moping round in exile because there was nothing to do and no altars to serve, Ezra was working away at his books till he became more skilled in Jewish law than all men, and, in Babylonian law, too, because Artaxerxes the king noticed him.

What is more, Ezra was possibly responsible for editing part of the Jewish scriptures as we know them. He may even have written that first magnificent chapter of Genesis: 'In the beginning God made the heavens and the earth, and the earth was without form and void. And darkness was upon the face of the deep.'

This means that Ezra was no recluse (and this is a third observation), no bespectacled, pale-faced, weedy book-worm unable to control men. Ezra, in spite of the stifling heat organised his fellow priests into a school of writers and raised their spirits by setting them to work, seeing clearly

something important—that if the Jewish religion
be centred on a building it could be centred on a boo
he who got that book written.

Fourthly, Ezra was a man of prayer. Some of tl
moving prayers in the Bible are in the book of Ezra, h
as it is of lists of names. Clearly Ezra was not only possessed
of a head but of a heart. That is why he stood out above all
men on the plains of Chebar. A singular man. A man who
was himself. A man who did not try to copy others. A man
who believed God had something for him to do. 'So,
knowing that the hand of the Lord my God was upon me, I
took courage.'

2 Ezra's courage

He certainly needed courage. He needed it because
Artaxerxes the king of Babylon picked him out, armed him
with an astonishing letter, a copy of which is in the Bible,
and despatched him to find out conditions in Jerusalem and
Judah and to set the country in order, making him almost the
king's plenipotentiary.

Ezra was no fool. He knew what he was in for. This task
would be no picnic. But he went. Years and years before a
whole batch of exiles had returned to their homeland under
Haggai and Zachariah. They had made a start at rebuilding,
but before long the whole situation deteriorated and morale
sank till society was foul. Then Ezra arrived and braced
himself for the task that lay before him. 'So, knowing that
the hand of the Lord my God was upon me, I took courage.'

3 Lessons from Ezra

What are the lessons from Ezra?

First, it is not the environment that is ultimately responsible
for what a man is, but how he reacts to that environment.
Hundreds of priests of good family and education malingered
in exile; one man, Ezra, turned it to good account.
Sometimes we say we will be this or do this when times are
favourable. If a man's spirit is right the times are always

avourable, yes, even this year crowded with many disappointments, frustrations and some things that make you sick. As a man's spirit is so is he. 'So, knowing that the hand of the Lord my God was upon me, I took courage.'

Second, Ezra was a man of the law. Ezra was a man of discipline. All the modern mood is to react against discipline. The promoters of a recent 'pop' festival said they were conducting an experiment in free living without the restraints of rules; upon which one newspaper in its second leader commented that the experiment was traceable back beyond Rousseau in France in the eighteenth century. Indeed, it is traceable further back, it is traceable back to the days of Ezra in the sixth century B.C. and the collapse of a society that tried to dispense with rules. Life will not hold together without discipline.

Thirdly, courage for being oneself, courage for being willing to differ from the crowd, courage for action deriving from a sense of God's hand upon us. The man of this faith is not weak but strong, not a man to sit around and be a drop-out, even mentally, but a man of action. ' . . . knowing that the hand of the Lord my God was upon me, I took courage . . . .'

Let us remind ourselves of one of the most astonishing and well-attested facts of history. It is the people who are most convinced of being instruments in God's hands that are the most active. It is as we believe that we belong to God the Eternal Father through Jesus Christ that we shall rise to our full stature 'So, knowing that the hand of the Lord my God was upon me, I took courage.'

18 GOD'S WORKMAN

Nehemiah 2.18 (NEB) *'So they set about the work vigorously.'*

Seated in the back seat of an empty down-town Church was a white-haired clergyman together with a much younger priest. They were deep in conversation and every now and again their eyes would turn to the ceiling, the walls and the ornamentation, for it had been a richly decorated building. That was the trouble, it was designed to be ornate but now it appeared faded and tired. This, however, was the Church of which the young man had been given sole charge—it was his first. The trouble was there was so much crying out to be done in the parish, where should he begin? 'If I were you', said the older man gently, and the younger one listened anticipating advice about visiting every house in the parish, or organising a campaign of spiritual renewal . . . . 'If I were you, first of all I should tackle the overgrown garden surrounding the Church, then the rusty ironwork of the ornamental gates, and then the notice boards (they need repainting, and not in black but in colour). Inside the building I should attempt one fairly big and obvious job which every one sees—what about that rood screen?' Twelve months later this man happened to be passing that same Church. Curiosity got the better of him and he had to stop and look. Every one of these jobs had been completed, and what was more significant, further enquiries elucidated the information that the life of that parish was on the up-grade.

In the Old Testament we are introduced to the father of all men who have to tackle a job in a situation that is dilapidated and depressing, and who have discovered the secret of where to begin. It is at some humble level which impinges on the ordinary life of the ordinary people who are connected with it. What is required first is not words but actions, not piety but practicality, not spirituality but humanity easily to be recognised. This may mean the cement-mixer, the paint-pot and gardening tools, and for a priest it may mean dungarees before a new chasuble. Nehemiah is the name of the man we shall examine.

Of course his book in the Old Testament (it is rather like a works diary) could be presented as a problem book. There are problems connected with it. Most ancient literature presents problems notably with regard to date and authorship. Here in this case it is whether the book of Ezra should precede that of Nehemiah or vice versa. There is strong evidence for the latter, but to allow the book of Nehemiah only to present problems is to fail lamentably with it. What we have is a striking picture of a strong man who knew what he was about. It is this which is able to become the very word of God to us.

1 *The man himself*

Who was Nehemiah? Nehemiah was an exile. He was not a priest but a layman. Specifically he was a cupbearer to the king in the land of his exile, a position of considerable eminence which gave him personal access to the royal presence; and that he had risen from a displaced person's camp to life at the court indicates that he must have possessed singular gifts in the way of personality, presentability and intellect. His elevation meant that, whether by compulsion or free choice, he had not returned to Jerusalem when his fellow-exiles were set free to do so. For all that, like many another Jew before and since, he could not put Jerusalem out of his mind. He asked permission to visit it when the news reached him of the miserable plight to which its inhabitants had been reduced because of the ruinous condition of the city walls and houses. The royal permission sought was granted and Nehemiah made the long trek across the burning deserts to see for himself.

What Nehemiah saw was a city completely demoralised. The German writers Heinrich Böll and Hans Bender have given us pictures of how their country appeared to German prisoners-of-war returning from Russia after perhaps seven, ten and even fifteen years in prisoner-of-war camps. They longed to feast their eyes on their home towns again, but when they actually saw them they scarcely recognised them, neither could they trace their families or pick up any old threads. And so gradually they drifted into lethargy, demoralisation, and very often crime. A man, a nation, can be in prison too long. After a while he disintegrates.

This is what took place for the exiles returning from Babylon to Jerusalem in 538 B.C. as a result of which all normal standards of living broke down. The people merely existed in hovels on the old city-site until Nehemiah arrived. Then the place began to be transformed. It was all done in a matter of weeks. What he accomplished is set out for us in the book that bears his name, accomplishments which cannot be detailed here but which (we should note), carry no suggestion of the miraculous, the visionary or the mystical. Everyone is down to earth. It is a story about walls, watch towers and weapons at the ready. No divine intervention was expected and none was given.

2 Lessons from the man

What has this story to say to people like ourselves?
At least three lessons.

First, that there are times when practical men of action are required more than visionaries, or to express this more exactly, there are times when what is required is men capable of translating visions into practical actions.

Secondly, the Church of God, whether the old Israel or the new Israel, has a proper place for various types of personality. Room must be provided for the visionary and also for the practical man, both belong to the one body. Jealousy, envy, or any despising of the one by the other, are therefore wrong.

Thirdly, Nehemiah reminds us of the place of a man's work in his life. A man's work is his dignity, or should be. Nehemiah prayed—do not fail to read Nehemiah's prayer in his book and to bear in mind that this activist was a man of prayer—and then he offered his work as his service of God. With Nehemiah it was not a case of *laborare est orare* (to work is to pray), it was *orare et laborare* (to pray *and* to work). This surely is man's highest achievement, and it makes a clear call especially to laymen in Church affairs.

There are various attitudes we can adopt towards our work. The poorest and least satisfying is to work for money's sake. Far better is it to work for the community's sake, but the best of all is to work for the community's sake for God's sake. This is the category to which Nehemiah's work belonged, and it must have included no small amount of desk-work, drudgery and dirtying of the hands.

In as much as we read this Jewish story with Christian eyes, we cannot help but remember that other Jew, Jesus of Nazareth, whom we call our Lord. He knew the smell of wood shavings, sawdust and glue. A carpenter has to be a precision worker, this craft requires the co-operation of hand, eye and brain. All this went into his work of redeeming mankind from the unpromising vantage point of occupied Palestine, till he was able to confess to God at the end, 'I have finished the work which thou gavest me to do.'

So there is set before us the ideal of God's workman. It could be any one of us. It should be every one of us. Temperament and type do not disqualify. Variety is needed in the household of God. Are you one of God's workmen? Do you see yourself as this in the ordinary occupation in which your life is set? You are or you are not God's workman, according to the motive which lies behind all you do. Is it for money's sake? Is it for the sake of the status you think it affords you? Is it for yourself? Your neighbour? Or for the sake of the community? The qualifying factor is whether or not any of this is done for God's sake. Nehemiah prompts the question.

19 THE GOD WHO GUIDES

Psalm 73.23 (NEB) *'Thou dost guide me by thy counsel and afterwards wilt receive me with glory.'*

INTRODUCTION

Among the various distinctive features of our age must be placed the vogue for 'doing it yourself'. The high cost of labour, and the difficulty of obtaining it for small jobs, has encouraged this amateur activity. 'Do it yourself', however, does not imply complete independence. A man may indeed dispense with the services of a paper-hanger when he undertakes the decoration of his sitting-room, but if he does not relish the sensation of utter frustration, or such a 'bodged job' that he cannot allow his friends to see inside his dwelling any more, he would be wise to buy a small book of instructions on the technique of paper-hanging, or watch some television 'Home Decoration' programme, or even attend evening classes. The truth is, there are few activities that can be accomplished successfully by the light of nature, we need guides and instructors for almost all the things we do in life.

This necessity covers the whole business of living. Civilisation is in fact the story of how people have learned to live not only efficiently but gracefully. Man has come a long way from the time when he lived in a cave to inhabiting a Palladian mansion or the Hilton Hotel in Park Lane.

But there are more matters about which we need guidance than building construction, lighting, heating and ventilation. What is the technique for dealing with a personal sense of inferiority? Is there a 'know-how' about living close to people with whose opinions you cannot possibly agree? What is the wrong line to take when a girl has jilted you? What attitude are we to adopt in the face of death? A man who does not seek a little plumbing advice before attempting to 'wipe a joint' on a lead pipe is a fool, and what shall we say of those who are so self-opinionated that they do not seek guidance on these far greater issues?

1 *The present*

In our text for today the Psalmist speaks out of personal experience—'Thou dost guide me by thy counsel', and he appends to it an indication of a further confidence which derives from it, 'and afterwards wilt receive me with glory.' 'Thou dost guide me by thy counsel.' Is this true? Does God guide us with his counsel? It cannot be proved in a court of law. Nowhere has God literally appeared to take anyone by the hand and say, 'This is the way, walk ye in it', 'turn not aside to the right hand nor to the left'; but there are people by the thousand ready to acknowledge that they felt they were being guided; and many thousands more who, looking back over a long life of fortune and achievement, are ready to discern a meaning in the strange windings of the road that have led them to the place where now they stand. One such confessor is the historian Charles Smyth, Fellow of Peterhouse, Cambridge, in a book called *Christian Friendship*.

(1) *Life style*

'Thou dost guide me by thy counsel.' There can be little doubt that the Psalmist meant by this what he called *The Torah*, which, loosely translated, means The Law, that is, the commandments and precepts written out in the Pentateuch and incorporated into the life of the nation. The faithful in Israel gloried in *The Torah*. It not only shaped the nation, but gave it stature and significance, lifting it above the level of the surrounding peoples. *The Torah* was, in fact, God's life-style for his people. This was the guide, this was the instruction, this was the benefactor of Israel, because it showed the way, not for its own sake, but for the profit of those who followed it.

'How dear are thy counsels unto me, O God:
O how great is the sum of them!'

(Psalm 139.17 BCP)

Is there here a permanent lesson for us who are not of the Jewish nation? Is there not a Christian life-style which will help a man at the uncertain turning-points of his earthly pilgrimage? Will it not help him to know that he belongs to a community that does not steal, does not fornicate, does not give false evidence, does not envy? This man will not stand dithering at the crossroads where temptation is strong—and we all reach those crossroads sooner or later; indeed, there is not much of a stretch on the road of life that is without such crossroads. The man, however, with a life-style negotiates them successfully and they do not really trouble him. Happy is the man with a life-style, and fortunate are the children who have such imparted to them. They know the truth of these words for themselves. 'Thou dost guide me by thy counsel.'

(2) Circumstances

God does not only guide, however, by a life-style. *The Torah* is not the only possession contained in the Old Testament for the welfare of God's people. God guides by circumstances. To deny this is to deny the very planking in the faith of Israel. The Hebrews staked their all on the belief that God had led them out of Egypt through the Red Sea. The waters were divided and beckoned the people to go forward with dry feet! 'This is the way, walk ye in it.' God guides by the opportunities and challenges that open up before us. Let the scholars probe, question and ask where and how the Exodus took place—and they are right to do so—what cannot be gainsaid is that Israel believed that God led them from bondage in Egypt to the freedom of the Promised Land. This belief is what made Israel 'tick' as she did. And the testimony of history is that those who believe they are divinely led through life are the ones whose lives are the most full of accomplishments. Curiously enough—or maybe it is not so curious—a belief in election does not produce indifference, but entirely the reverse!

(3) Persons

And God guides by providing leaders in the shape of persons. The Old Testament is very definite about this. God called Moses, took David from the sheep-fold and constrained Jeremiah against his will to be his prophet. God did not simply open up the Red Sea and let it beckon, he sent a man to lead his people through. Such was Israel's faith about the past, and such was Isaiah's message for the future.

> ' . . . and a man shall be a refuge from the wind
> and a shelter from the tempest,
> or like runnels of water in dry ground,
> like the shadow of a great rock in a thirsty land.'
>
> (Isaiah 32.2 NEB)

And who is there so insensitive that he does not know this to be true? Where would some of us be today without that parent we did not choose who 'trained us up in the way we should go'? Or that school teacher who took trouble over us? Or that clergyman who, noting our potentiality, saw that it was given an opportunity to develop? God brings people into our lives for our temporal good, which the Old Testament would call our 'salvation'. And they are not all obvious people in positions of authority, but friends, of both sexes, husbands, wives . . .

> 'How dear are thy counsels unto me O God:
> O how great is the sum of them!'

2 The future

God guides by his counsels contained in the life-style he has proclaimed, he guides by circumstances which beckon us to go forward, and he guides through the agency of people he brings into our lives for his own specific purposes. But this is not the conclusion of the matter. How could it reasonably be? Is there not our final frontier we all must approach called death? What happens there? Does the guide fail us at this moment? Does he lose interest at this crisis, the greatest crisis of all, even failing to appear, not caring at all whether we survive the ordeal or make any provision for what lies beyond?

Think of a trainer of two skating champions at the Streatham Ice Rink. Does she go through weeks and weeks, months and months, even years of coaching, reproving and encouraging, getting her trainees through one championship and now another, only to fail them altogether when they appear for the great contest at the Olympic Games? Is she not in the grandstand willing their victory, ready to acknowledge and contribute to their glory?

The very fact that God guides his servants now is evidence that he will guide us then. God could not be God, that is, not the righteous and true God, if he abandoned us at the last of life's hurdles. Of course it is true, as every careful student of the Old Testament knows, that there is no explicit indisputable doctrine of a life to come beyond the grave in any of its contents but God's guidance in the here and now so implies and infers his guidance over death that the hope of life on the other side cannot let itself be stifled.

'Thou dost guide me by thy counsel
and afterwards wilt receive me with glory'

And if we phrase this in the shape of a question, if we label it as expressing man's longing, then the answer of the New Testament is a plain 'yes': Yes, you think God must, in the nature of things, guide you safely through the last gate if he has guided you through all those lesser gates. Yes, Christ is your confirmation. He has gone through the gate of death himself and opened it wide. This is our exodus, and he is our leader, waiting for us on the other side.

'Thou dost guide me by thy counsel
and afterwards wilt receive me with glory.'

20 AN OLD TESTAMENT BEATITUDE

Psalm 84.5 (BCP) *'Blessed is the man whose strength is in thee'*

In the book of Judges is a crude story about a strong man. We do the story no service and we do the Old Testament no favour if we attempt to spiritualise it, allegorise it or seek for 'types' in it, thereby hoping to refine it. It cannot be refined no matter what elegance of literary style Milton might employ to retell it. Samson, the subject, was crude, coarse and cunning, with little religion as we understand it, and the tales that were told of him, we may guess, have lost nothing in the telling, especially in the circles where no doubt they circulated. A hired girl wheedling her way into a man's secret at the instigation of a foreign power! What a story for the vulgar press! And how easily in our intellectual and moral superiority we may miss the message of this man's portrait painted with such garish pigments. The source of Samson's strength was not obvious. This is the message. The

75

secret of Samson's strength did not lie on the surface. This is the message. It was in fact grounded in a vow of dedication to God who had chosen him. So for all his crudity and all his buffoonery, Samson was in this one respect a true son of Israel whose strength lay in her special relationship to God alone. So in a dark day this underlying faith of Israel was somehow caught in the mirror of this crude man's crude life, reflecting it back for all with eyes to see that a person's strength can be in God, a truth which the Psalmist poured into the refinement of poetry when he sang,

'Blessed is the man whose strength is in thee: in whose heart are thy ways.
Who going through the vale of misery use it for a well: and the pools are filled with water.'

1 *Hidden strength*

Not quite twenty years ago I met the wife of one of the Admirals who fought in the battle of Jutland. She was one of the strongest characters it has been my privilege to encounter. She certainly did not appear strong, on the contrary, she looked frail being then over seventy. She had a beautiful face and was strikingly refined in style and conversation. But she was strong. I never knew her overcome. She had her full share of troubles. Her first husband was drowned in the Titanic; and it must be said that her heartbreaking sorrows had impressed a certain sadness on her eyes. But she was never bitter, never resentful, never depressed. One Christmas time, when over eighty and alone in her flat, the water tank burst. No plumber was available on Christmas Day and she fell down in the water. Yet even this she recounted as a funny story. Nor shall I forget how, time and time again, she would enquire what books I had read lately, and if I floundered she would outline some of the latest stiff biographies she had mastered. Mastered! Yes, this is the right word, she had mastered life. She was strong, even when her physical life was ebbing away, she was strong in spirit, as I saw eight days before she died. Her secret lay in what this text describes,

'Blessed is the man whose strength is in thee' indeed, the whole verse as it proceeds,

'Blessed is the man whose strength is in thee: in whose heart are thy ways.
Who going through the vale of misery use it for a well: and the pools are filled with water.'

This subtle concept of strength, not physical and not obvious, the complete counterpart of those extraordinary looking individuals sometimes seen on television in weight-lifting championships, huge men with huge muscles, is reflected in the Bible. Samson displayed none of the outward manifestations of superior strength, neither did David in another Old Testament story, indeed he was puny in comparison with Goliath of Gath, who, according to the tale about him, stood over nine feet wielding a spear more like a weaver's beam, whereas David was young, lithe and handsome. Discerning men, however, could not fail to notice David's head and David's bearing, all of which Michelangelo caught in the marble of his marvellous statue in the *Accademia* in Florence. The truth is strength can derive from an inner principle of life so that those who appear weak may in fact be strong, so strong that they accomplish more in life than do the majority, so strong that none of the calamities that affect us all throw them down. Such is the picture of him whom the text describes, 'Blessed is the man whose strength is in thee.'

Perhaps this truth of hidden strength derived from an inner principle of life has not often been embodied more strikingly than in the story of Edith Cavell, arrested by the German army in Belgium in November 1914 for assisting British soldiers trapped behind the enemy lines to escape across the Dutch frontier, court-martialled and finally shot. Her fifty-year long life only acquired dramatic proportions at the end, but what proportions they were! To see her in the greyness of that early morning walking with her accustomed dignity from her death-cell along the corridor out to that stake in the ground where she was tied, blindfolded and shot, was unforgettable to those who witnessed it. And when they took away the corpse and removed the bandages from her striking face, it was noticed that she must have cried before the bullets struck. But this was all. 'Patriotism is not enough,' she had said, and her words remain today in an age when we are witnessing terrible deeds done in the name of nationalism. But Edith Cavell, third daughter of the Vicar of Swardeston, three miles from Norwich, gently bred, was a strong woman who lived by principle. It was evident in her high cheek-boned face, evident even to escaped soldiers on the run who had reason to be thankful for her courage in face of every threat, and called her 'angel'. 'Blessed is the man/woman whose strength is in thee.' There is nothing with which it is comparable. It is strength in weakness, standing in a class by itself. It is a strength open to us all.

2 Strength through joy

And now the second part of this Old Testament beatitude, '. . . in whose heart are thy ways'. The Hebrew here for 'ways' means 'highways' or 'pilgrim ways', and the picture is of companies of people journeying up to Jerusalem to worship in the temple at one of the annual festivals. These were happy occasions. The participants sang as they went. Not that the journey was all that comfortable, sometimes quite the reverse, but they knew where they were going and what was the purpose of their enterprise. It was to worship on Mount Zion, the place where pre-eminently God dwelt, the God who had rescued them from Egypt, and given them their land, the God from whom they derived all that was worth having in life. So their hearts were set up, or lifted up, on the highways of Zion (see the *Revised Psalter*, 1966), because they knew where they were going, they had a sense of direction, the very opposite of people who have lost their way.

Is this not a large part of our trouble in the 1970s, we have no pilgrim way? We do not see life as a pilgrimage. To thousands upon thousands life is no more than 'one damn thing after another'. It doesn't come from anywhere, and it doesn't go anywhere. This is partly why we are weak. This is why we have lost our buoyancy. This is why we are bored. These men and women mirrored in Psalm 84 were strong because they were happy, and they were happy because they were going somewhere, or in the words of a song from a generation less sophisticated than ours:

> 'We're marching to Zion,
> Beautiful, beautiful Zion.
> We're marching homeward to Zion,
> That beautiful city of God'

In Germany during the years before the second world war, a deliberate policy was undertaken to foster strength through joy. *Kraft durch Freude*. This was the motto. And there was truth in what those Nazi leaders attempted, which is why Germany became formidable. People are stronger if they are joyful. They weaken if they are depressed. But how can they be made joyful? Will entertainment suffice? Will a political programme answer to the requirements? Does there not need to be faith, faith which reaches out and beyond the boundaries of this life and applies to the changes and chances within it as well? Jesus of Nazareth possessed such a faith. He believed in spite of the cruel death he knew must be his lot. Of him, therefore, the writer of the Epistle to the Hebrews in the New Testament wrote ' . . . who for the joy that was set before him endured the cross, despising the shame' (Hebrews 12.2 RV) That is to say, Jesus was strong because of his joy, and Jesus was joyous because of his faith.

3 *Strength through suffering*

And now we come to the difficult part of the two verses from which the text was taken, difficult to see its plain meaning, difficult to accept what it teaches. 'Who going through the vale of misery use it for a well: and the pools are filled with water.'

Go back in imagination to those pilgrims on the road to worship at the temple on Mount Zion. The journey for many of them, especially those from the north, had been long and arduous. Some of the way was pleasant, some of it across grim desert wastes, hard to bear. And when they were almost at journey's end, a particularly arduous trek was necessary. It led, according to Renan (*Vie de Jesus*, Ch. iv), through a narrow and gloomy valley called *Ain el-Haramija*, where, out of the rocks in which graves were cut, there flowed dark and blackish water. This may have been so. Of this, however, we can be certain, this stage of the pilgrim's journey was repellent. But they persevered. They pushed on. Indeed, the very toughness of the way toughened their resolve. Because they journeyed with firm purpose they even acquired strength through their sufferings, all the more remarkable for coming towards the end of their journey when any traveller would be expected to be weakened by his efforts. This is what the Psalm reflects in the verse which follows, 'They will go from strength to strength.'

Does suffering automatically produce an increase of strength? The answer is no. Suffering by itself is a frightening, weakening, debilitating experience, only even bearable if it is linked with purpose. 'Why must I suffer this?' cries the patient in the hospital to the chaplain who visits him. 'Tell me, chaplain, just give me one reason and I will stick it out.' Or the comment from the next bed in the ward, 'All right, padre, I guess it's for some reason I'm getting punishment.' Crude comments? Of course they are crude, but they carry the underlying truth that we can endure suffering if we sense in it a purpose, and then it strengthens us. So the phrase can stand—strength through suffering.

* * *

Is this Psalm full of psychological insight? It is indeed. There is such a phenomenon in human personality as hidden strength. It is true that a joyous spirit nourishes strength and a depressed spirit fosters debility. It is true that strength derives, not from coddling but from exposure to roughness; but—and this is the new preaching from the Old Testament—only when our faces confidently (which means with faith) are turned towards God, whom it is our joy to worship. Worship has largely dropped out of modern living, which loss may indicate one reason why we are so weak. Worship has largely been soft-pedalled in mid-twentieth century Christianity, replacing service of God by service of man, and then, as Evelyn Underhill said, religion does not wear well. The opening verses of Psalm 84 set the key.

'O how amiable are thy dwellings: thou Lord of hosts! My soul hath a desire and longing to enter into the courts of the Lord: my heart and my flesh rejoice in the living God'

Out of this joyous, faithful worship, strength derives, or as the text expresses it,

'Blessed is the man whose strength is in thee'

21 NO, MR PREACHER

Ecclesiastes 12.13 *'Fear God, and keep his commandments: for this is the whole duty of man.'*

I am sorry, Mr Preacher, but I can't agree with you. I know your words are in the Bible, I know this saying of yours is in the Bible, 'Fear God, and keep his commandments: for this is the whole duty of man.' I respect you. I honour you. With but a little persuasion you would make me your disciple for I know no place in the Old Testament where the language is more moving or more expressive than in the book of Ecclesiastes where you have written; but I have to part company with you, though I do so with regret.

1 *Attractions*

First, let me confess why you attract me. You attract me because you are ill at ease in the world. No, not because you are cold or naked, or hungry or thirsty, or in prison, quite the reverse. Everything seems to have gone your way. You have run to the limits as a hedonist—wine, women and song—what have you left out? Fine houses, fine gardens, pools of water—you have experienced them all. And you did not stop at superficialities, you bent your head over your books, you did more than walk around your libraries, you imbibed the wisdom stored therein. You are no lightweight, no inexperienced, uneducated buffoon, but a serious pursuer after excellence. Yes, you attract me for the way you have entered into life, drinking of all that it offers to the full. Yet you still feel dissatisfied. That is why you attract me. 'Emptiness or emptiness,' saith the Preacher, 'everything is empty.'

I suppose I shall have to label you as a cynic, but I do so without distaste. No clod is a cynic. The sows guzzling up the swill in their troughs are never cynics. They possess no fine feelings to be frustrated. But a man who is a cynic betrays the hurt that he has experienced in life. He is a man with a sensitive skin for the protection of which he wears his cynicism like a garment. Gladly he would go without it, but after the things that he has suffered he cannot do so with impunity.

Secondly, you attract me, Mr Preacher, because you have so strong a sense of beauty in this world. Of God you say, 'He hath made everything beautiful in his time', and like the classical writers and sculptors you possess a marvellous sense of proportion: and beauty largely consists in proportion. 'There is', you say,

> 'a time to be born, and a time to die;
> a time to plant, and a time to pluck up that which is planted;
> a time to kill, and a time to heal;
> a time to break down, and a time to build up;
> a time to weep, and a time to laugh;
> a time to mourn, and a time to dance;
> a time to cast away stones, and a time to gather stones together;
> a time to embrace, and a time to refrain from embracing;
> a time to get, and a time to lose;
> a time to keep, and a time to cast away;
> a time to rend, and a time to sew;
> a time to keep silence, and a time to speak;
> a time to love, and a time to hate;
> a time of war, and a time of peace.'

Your sense of proportion has given you a sense of time in the way the Greeks used their word *kairos*, the fit time, as opposed to clock-time, *chronos*. So you are a philosopher as well as an artist, or rather a philosopher because you are a supreme artist, for there can be no great artist lacking a philosophy of human existence.

Thirdly, you attract me because you are a wise old man full of years and full of experience, and I love to sit at your feet and hear you talk. It is no wonder your words have been enshrined in what the Hebrews called their wisdom literature.

'Better is a handful with quietness, than both hands full with travail and vexation of spirit.

Better is a poor and a wise child than an old and foolish king, who will no more be admonished.

For out of prison he cometh to reign; whereas also he that is born to a kingdom becometh poor.

The sleep of the labouring man is sweet, whether he eat little or much: but the abundance of the rich will not suffer him to sleep.

It is better to hear the rebuke of the wise, than for a man to hear the song of fools.

For as the crackling of thorns under a pot, so is the laughter of a fool: this also is vanity.

Be not hasty in thy spirit to be angry: for anger resteth in the bosom of fools.'

Repeatedly you employ the word wisdom in your book of Ecclesiastes, and wisdom is of so much more value than cleverness. A farm labourer can be a wise man and a doctor of science a fool, for the first man learns how to adjust to life, and the second imagines he can bend it to his will.

2 Pity

Yet for all my admiration of you, Mr Preacher, still I pity you. What has come your way that you should write,

'A good name is better than precious ointment; and the day of death than the day of one's birth.

It is better to go to the house of mourning, than to the

house of feasting: for that is the end of all men; and the
living will lay it to his heart.
Sorrow is better than laughter: for by the sadness of
countenance the heart is made better'?

And what bitterness must you have known for you to tell this
story—

'There was a little city, and few men within it; and there
came a great king against it, and besieged it, and built
great bulwarks against it;
Now there was found in it a poor wise man, and he by his
wisdom delivered the city; yet no man remembered that
same poor man.'

If you have a sense of justice in life, Mr Preacher, and I know
you have, I can understand how you have become a cynic.
With the world as you have seen it, goodness does not always
seem to profit.

3 *Disagreement*

So what is your theology? What is your doctrine of God, and
of man, and of the relation between them both? This is the
point where I must leave your company. You say, and
rightly say of God, 'He hath made everything beautiful in his
time', and you go on to state of men and women—'also he
hath set eternity in their heart.' Yes, I agree. Possessions do
not permanently satisfy. Somehow there is a longing in the
human heart for something more. It is this which great music
and great painting poignantly proclaim. In some sense man is
a displaced person in this world for he carries an eternal
dimension in his inner self—O, Mr Preacher, you have come
a long way with your book of Ecclesiastes as compared with
the book of Judges in the Old Testament, but I think you
have missed the path as regards your understanding of God,
or you would never say that God has made everything
beautiful and has set eternity in man's heart in order that no
man can find out the work that God maketh from the
beginning to the end. God is not one who purposely blinds

our eyes so that he can retain his own inscrutibility. I do not wonder, Mr Preacher, that you have found life so empty a show if this is all you know of God. Do you not understand how God, out of love for mankind reveals himself? Does not the redemption of Israel from Egypt say anything to you about your own day-to-day experience? God is the hidden God, yes! And the transcendent God, yes! But is he not also 'the Father who pitieth his own children; for he knoweth our frame, he remembereth that we are but dust'?

So I have to disagree with you, Mr Preacher,—and I shall not be the first or the last to disagree with a preacher—I shall have to disagree with you when you end your book with the sentence, 'Let us hear the conclusion of the matter: Fear God, and keep his commandments: for this is the whole duty of man.' God is not primarily the Judge, but primarily the Redeemer. God loves us, and has made himself known to us and given us the sense of being guided by his hand. This is what takes away the meaninglessness of life, replacing it with realisation of divine purpose. Everything is not empty. Agnosticism is not the sole possible viewpoint for life. We are not left with nothing but blind duty as our principle of living. We can rise up with a warm answering love to the self-sacrificing love of God bestowed upon us.

Is it that you cannot know this, Mr Preacher, as we can know it in the good news of our Saviour, Jesus Christ? Is it that you have taken us as far as you can without this knowledge and what you have achieved makes Christ shine as a light even brighter still? Untruth is not what you have given us, Mr Preacher, else it would scarcely stand within the Canon of the Scriptures, but limited truth, truth about life apart from Christ. So we thank you for your message and for the noble sensitivity of the human spirit you have shown us apart from Christ, enhancing the dignity of man; but do not blame us if we run to Christ for the answer to your book, for we believe that you, too, would find in him your satisfaction.

22 FAITHFULNESS

Jeremiah 1.17 & 19 (NEB) *'Brace yourself, Jeremiah; stand up and speak to them. . . for I am with you and will keep you safe.'*

You will groan when you note the subject of this sermon, everyone who knows no better groans when he hears of Jeremiah, reckoning that he must steel himself for an entry into misery. After all, has not the English language a word derived from his name, that is, jeremiad. We exclaim over a pessimist's foreboding—what a jeremiad! How can we suffer it! What a dismal prospect!—And always with the implication that the speaker has exaggerated the darkness. Having no light in himself he sees no light on any horizon.

But ought we to write off Jeremiah in this summary fashion? Can the book that bears his name which is so fine a piece of literature that Green, the French novelist, learnt Hebrew in order to appreciate its finer points, can it have no more effect on us than to produce a groan? Is it not true that Jeremiah is one of the finest if not the finest of all the Old Testament characters? Where will you find a more sensitive man than Jeremiah, or a more courageous man, or a more faithful man? Do not forget that when these three characteristics occur together greatness exists. 'Man!', sneered one infantry man to another, groping his way on patrol out into the dangerous darkness of 'No Man's Land', 'You are terrified, shaking in every limb.' 'Yes,' came the reply, 'and if you were half as afraid as I am, you would have quitted long ago.'

1 *Faithful to the call to service*

Jeremiah did not wish to be a prophet of the Lord. This is worth noting well because we ought to be chary about anyone who 'bends over backwards' to enter the official ministry. Pay more attention to the reluctant preacher. He is not in the job for what he can get out of it. He is no one who merely loves the sound of his own voice. His aim is not set

upon status, position or authority. Pay attention to Jeremiah.
The last thing he looked for was publicity. Indeed he hated
the idea and shrank from it. Jeremiah was a countryman, that
is to say, a countryman with eyes for the lonely sights of the
wide open spaces near his home at Anathoth, north of
Jerusalem. He observed the sky, the wild animals, the
migratory birds, their habits and their cries. Jeremiah was
solitary who loved nothing so much as to capture the
sublimities of the world of nature in exquisite descriptive
poetry. What attraction could the foeted alleyways of the
capital city hold for such a man as this? And had not his
remote ancestor Adonijah in the time of Solomon, meddled
in political manoeuvres enough to discourage his descendents
for ever from trying their hand again No, Jeremiah wanted
nothing of the rôle of a public figure in Israel. Anyway, he
was too young and hopeless (so he thought), as a public
speaker.

But God called him. He called him by means of the
unlikely signs of an almond tree in blossom and an overturned
pot balanced above the crackling flames. But Jeremiah was
accustomed to hear words spoken by events in the natural
order. And they became 'word-events', as the Germans say,
but how terrifying was their command on this occasion! It
was a call to prophesy to the nations 'to pull down and to
uproot, to destroy and to demolish, to build and to plant.'

'Brace yourself, Jeremiah:' (said the voice),
'stand up and speak to them.
Tell them everything I bid you,
do not let your spirit break at sight of them,
or I will break you before their eyes.
This day I make you a fortified city,
a pillar of iron, a wall of bronze,
to stand fast against the whole land,
against the kings and princes of Judah,
its priests and its people.
They will make war on you but shall not overcome you,
for I am with you and will keep you safe.
This is the very word of the Lord.'

No man ever entered a pulpit more reluctantly and with knees knocking more than did Jeremiah, prophet of the Lord.

2 Faithful under persecution

And the people laughed at him when they heard him. No, not because he was a comic figure or a stumbling speaker lacking skill with language. Quite the reverse. His audiences smarted under his tongue. Who would not? Listen to him:

> 'Your sons have forsaken me and sworn by gods
> that are no gods.
> I gave them all they needed, yet they preferred adultery,
> and haunted the brothels;
> each neighs after another man's wife,
> like a well-fed and lusty stallion.
> Shall I not punish them for this?
> the Lord asks.'

There is laughter at the comic and this is touched with pathos indicating sympathy. All the world's great clowns understand this and work on it, not least Sir Charles Chaplin. But there is laughter which conceals hatred and takes the form of mockery. Always respect a man who is mocked. It means the people fear his power. Jesus was mocked. Jeremiah was mocked.

> 'I have been made a laughing-stock all the day long,
> everyone mocks me.
> Whenever I speak I must needs cry out
> and proclaim violence and destruction.
> I am reproached and mocked all the time
> for uttering the word of the Lord.'

But Jeremiah persevered in spite of the mockery. This is the point to register. He was faithful under persecution and this is what mockery is—persecution. Yes, from the gang of schoolboys in the playground mocking a junior for keeping his word, to a hospital ward where a patient is laughed at for taking the Sacrament. Ridicule and mockery are the contemporary instruments of torture for Christians. Dare we be faithful? This is the question this subject poses.

But Jeremiah had more than words to suffer. There were deeds as well, that day when his hearers stuffed him down in an empty water cistern which was not empty. That was the terror. Better to drown in a matter of minutes than to linger for days in the slime at the bottom. And Jeremiah sank in it, and the cover, you may guess, was replaced at the entrance. Who would have it in his heart to blame Jeremiah if at that moment he renounced his rôle of the prophet of the Lord? But he was rescued, hauled up by a black man, with ropes and old clouts of rags under his arm-pits. And then we see him standing in the royal presence, King Zedekiah taking careful measure of Jeremiah and Jeremiah taking careful measure of King Zedekiah, both afraid, but both courageous, each with a distasteful duty to perform which the other recognised, evoking respect. We saw the like between the Commandant of Colditz and the Colonel in charge of the British prisoners in the television presentation. Jeremiah was steadfast under physical persecution as also under mockery.

3 Faithful under disappointment

Thirdly, Jeremiah was faithful under disappointment. The people would not heed his counsel. They blinded their eyes to the signs of the times in which they lived. They refused to recognise the might of Babylon, hankering without reason for the assistance of Egypt. And so the blow fell, the blow Jeremiah had prophesied. Nebuchadnezzar reduced Jerusalem to a heap of stones, among which the riff-raff eked out their perilous existence because the enemy had deported only the top people from the conquered country. Among those left was Jeremiah, a lonely survivor of the upper classes. But he did not desert his headstrong, rebellious, defeated people. He stayed in Jerusalem. And when contrary to all advice, this motley remnant trekked to Egypt, he took the road among them. His compatriots had made a mess of life before the invasion and they made a mess of it immediately after. They murdered Gedaliah, a reasonable governor, appointed by

Babylon, and would not take Jeremiah's advice to stay in the land. So the last we hear of Jeremiah is at Tahpanhes in Egypt, staying with this disappointing people. But Jeremiah was no stranger to disappointment. He had lived through the futility of Josiah's reformation and he had seen the scroll of his written prophecies cut up with a knife and dropped into the fire by the king's own hand. Yet Jeremiah never parted company with his people.

The Church which Jeremiah served was not the last to disappoint. The Catholic Church, the Reformed Church, and even the local church we know, has each one brought its disappointments. Sometimes there has been downright evil, more often mere uninspiring unimaginative dullness. What then should its adherents do? Of Jeremiah we read that he never left his people. He was faithful under disappointment.

What was the end of this man? We do not know. Presumably he died in Egypt, the land of bondage for his forebears. But his message did not die. And what was it? It was a message of hope. 'The days will come,' he said, 'when God will make a new covenant with his people'—And those days arrived. They arrived with Jesus of Nazareth. They arrived when he broke bread and poured out wine the night before his death, saying, 'This is my blood, the blood of the new covenant shed for many . . . ' No wonder his disciples when asked on an earlier occasion whom the crowds thought he was, replied, 'Some say you are Jeremiah!' Jesus and Jeremiah are very close the one to the other. Both addressed men by their words, their deeds and their deaths, faithful throughout. This is the lesson of Jeremiah, not a dismal jeremiad, but an arresting call to faithfulness to our high calling whatever the mockery, whatever the disappointment.

> 'Brace yourself, Jeremiah;
> stand up and speak to them. . . .
> for I am with you and will keep you safe.'

23 GOD'S NEW ALLIANCE

Jeremiah 31.31 (NEB) ' . . . *I will make a new covenant . . .* '

Shortly before the outbreak of war in 1939, Germany suddenly announced an alliance with Russia. The news broke upon an astonished world, for had not Germany been notorious for her denunciation of Russia, hating its Communism? What then lay behind this diplomatic move? The alliance was certainly not motivated by mutual love! Political alliances are rarely, if ever, motivated by mutual love! Their purpose is to adjust the balance of power for aggressive or defensive aims. So Britain allied with Portugal against Napoleon, and one hundred years later with France against Kaiser Wilhelm II.

Nor are company alliances born of mutual love. It was not for this reason that the Westminster Bank joined with the National Provincial, but to increase capital and to increase power.

1 *An alliance in love*

The Old Testament, however, tells of a different kind of alliance—God's alliance with men. The proclamation of it constitutes the good news of the Old Testament. It is wholly unlike a political alliance and wholly unlike a business merger, because it really is based on love. It is rooted in God's personal choice.

Perhaps the best illustration in the Old Testament is to be found in the story of David and Jonathan. Jonathan was a prince in King Saul's (his father's) court, and David was a shepherd boy. He was introduced there to soothe the king's melancholy by playing on his harp. Little obvious advantage would accrue to Jonathan by allying himself with David, either at the outset, or later on when David's qualities became so apparent, even to the king, that the king became dangerous with jealousy. But Jonathan did not waver. He was drawn to David. Even when his father was bent on killing David, he did not change his course. David and Jonathan were in fact knit together in the closest bond of personal devotion. It was an alliance based on mutual love, the ultimate depth of which was apparent when David crossed those terrible slopes of Mount Gilboa after a bloody battle with the Philistines, and there, mutilated among the corpses, was heaped the body of his friend. So then as now, the depth of our love comes home to us when we watch those crematorium doors close upon the earthly remains of one we knew we cared about, but not till then how deeply.

> 'I grieve for you, Jonathan my brother;
> dear and delightful you were to me;
> your love for me was wonderful,
> surpassing the love of women.'
>
> (2 Samuel 1.26 NEB)

When God makes an alliance with men, it is in those terms that he makes it. There is no aggressive or defensive aim. It seeks no increase of power or resources. God, because he is God, is sufficient in himself, but he chooses men, takes them into his alliance, and makes it binding with sacrifice.

2 God's old alliance with Israel

The Old Testament tells the story of God's alliance with men and how it centred first upon the nation of Israel beginning with the deliverance from Egypt. It was an alliance motivated by love with no ulterior aims, but it was an alliance; that is to say, although it was in no sense a bargain between God and men, there were two sides to it. And one side could be faithful and the other side could be faithless, as in a marriage. Indeed, the Old Testament employs one whole book in its collection, the book of Hosea, to take a broken marriage as an illustration of Israel's unfaithfulness to the alliance God had made with it at Sinai.

This really is the overriding, all-important belief which made Israel what it was, that at Sinai, after the deliverance from the slavery of Egypt, God did choose to make an alliance with this people, who for their part, were bidden to keep his commandments. But they failed. They trailed after other gods. They began to imagine that their own skill and sagacity had brought them to the state of nationhood, forgetting all about the deliverance from Egypt and the pact at Sinai. All in all, this is the story the Old Testament has to tell, of God choosing to ally himself with a people and calling for faithfulness, but also of that people slipping out of the alliance to their own ultimate hurt.

And now the time has come to substitute for the word alliance, the technical word which the Bible employs for God's alliance—namely, *covenant*. So Exodus 34.10, one of the earliest accounts of what happened at Sinai reads, 'The Lord said, "Here and now I make a covenant." ' And we can go on to summarize in the words of Jeremiah what happened to that covenant in the past, and what would happen in the future, a message of disappointment and a message of hope. ' "The time is coming," ' says the Lord, "when I will make a new covenant with Israel and Judah. It will not be like the covenant I made with their forefathers when I took them by the hand and led them out of Egypt. Although they broke my covenant, I was patient with them," says the Lord, "But this is the covenant which I will make with Israel after those days," says the Lord, "I will set my law within them and write it on their hearts ... for I will forgive their wrongdoing and remember their sin no more." ' (Jeremiah 31.31–34 NEB)

3 *The new alliance*

So centuries of the story of God's alliance slip away and we find ourselves peering through a doorway into an upstairs room. Twelve men sit at table overcome with foreboding. Tomorrow their host, to whom they are devoted, will suffer the ultimate penalty of capital punishment in its cruellest form—crucifixion, and by the cruellest means—betrayal. But he takes bread and breaks it, lifts a cup of wine and passes it round, saying 'This is my body ... this is my blood of the new covenant,' (the new alliance), 'which is given for you; do this in remembrance of me.'

God made an alliance with Israel at Sinai, this is the preaching of the Old Testament, the old covenant. God in Christ made an alliance with all men in an upper room at Jerusalem the night before his death. This is the preaching of the New Testament, the new covenant. More accurately, it is the new preaching from the Old Testament, because the new is built upon the old. But like all good preaching it demands a verdict. Each individual, each generation, has to answer for itself. A question is posed by the proclamation of God's alliance with men, a question with supplementaries. Do we recognise the alliance? Do we accept it? Do we set our ultimate security in it? Are we faithful for our part to this alliance? The story of Israel could be my story. It could be my generation's story. God has proclaimed his new alliance at Christ's cross and resurrection with all men. He has let it be symbolised in the Holy Communion. 'This is my body . . . this is my blood of the new covenant' (the new alliance). Am I a party to this? Do I understand what is involved both of responsibility and of privilege? Do I rest myself here? These are the really great questions.

24 REBUILDING IS POSSIBLE

Amos 7.7 (NEB) *'There was a man standing by a wall with a plumb-line in his hand.'*

Amos must have seen this sight more than once. Maybe he had stood himself on occasions with a plumb-line in his own hand. Perhaps he had constructed a shelter for those cattle he herded. Men were forced to turn their hands to all manner of occupations if they were to make a living in the eighth century B.C. in Judaea, which is why in the hot, dry season Amos made his way down to the coastal plain to dress sycamore trees. That he also understood the uses of a plumb-line is therefore likely. Probably he had actually built walls as well as driven cows to market and bargained for them in Bethel.

A plumb-line is necessary in any building operation to test the uprightness of the walls while the various courses of stones or bricks are being superimposed the one on top of the other, because if the walls are not true, the corners of the building cannot be constructed and the roofing will not fit.

1 *Eighth century crookedness*

In the eighth century B.C. a new society was growing up in the kingdom of Israel and Judah. It was an age of relative prosperity compared with the previous century. This was partly due to a time of unprecedented peace enjoyed by the whole community. Both Philistia and Syria, Israel's hostile neighbours, had passed the zenith of their power and were no longer harassing the Israel borders, and Assyria, the deadly foe of the future, had not yet marshalled her forces, nor begun to lust after western lands.

But what was Israel doing with her peace? She was building up her material resources, and improving the living standards of her people—a laudable aim. The Hebrew people have never developed propensities towards asceticism nor undervalued the benefits to be derived from material welfare. Prosperity was even counted as an index of the good hand of God upon life, which was to be enjoyed richly and unashamedly. When however Amos employed his plumb-line he found the walls of his contemporary society anything but true. Bribery and corruption abounded, the wealthy filling their pockets at the expense of the poor. There was luxury and laziness, cheating in the market place, annexation of land by underhand dealings, people tricked out of their possessions so that they were forced to sell their labour at a cheaper rate for the enrichment of the already rich. So the balance of society was becoming distorted, with class war poisoning the whole.

It was the application of his moral plumb-line that made Amos a prophet. He came to it when one day he saw with new eyes what he had seen a hundred times before, 'a man standing by a wall with a plumb-line in his hand'. From then on there burned into his soul the conviction that God stands with his plumb-line testing the walls of society whether in Israel, Judah, Tyre, Edom, Britain or America, and if those walls are not true, that society will not be safely constructed, indeed, it faces eventual collapse.

2 Twentieth century crookedness

Is there any escape for our society from the application of the plumb-line? Perhaps we are of the opinion that no plumb-line exists. There are no external measuring lines by which the soundness of a nation's social and community life may be tested, that is to say, no measuring lines that can be universally applied! Conduct is relative to the historical period in which it is carried out. What is right for one age may be wrong for another; and not only relative to time but to place. There is a right for one part of the globe and another right for another. In other words there are no absolute standards of right and wrong for a community universally applicable. With such a view the prophet Amos profoundly disagreed. God, he says, is a God of social justice and wherever and whenever this is flouted, he is flouted and judgement ensues.

Is our present society out of alignment? Would Amos' plumb-line, would God's plumb-line, indicate that the walls of Britain today are not straight? What is the most obvious defect? Is it not selfishness? There is the childish form of selfishness, the form in which grown men and women seek to grab as much as they can of the good things of life regardless of the underprivileged, the unfortunate, the powerless and the infirm, their minds set on food, drink, comfort and pleasure. The incidence of obesity in the powerful Western lands is one of the most terrible indictments of selfishness in a world where hunger is the experience of the greater part of mankind. Too many people do not care so long as they get what they want. The plumb-line revels a selfishness as crude as this.

But selfishness also on a massive scale. By means of a steady process of increasing knowledge throughout the last four hundred years, awesome now in its sheer magnitude, the scientific method has equated matter and energy, placing in human hands a mastery of the world's resources inconceivable throughout the greater part of human history. From two opposites—minute atoms to vast torrents of energy man has learnt the ultimate nature of physical reality. And what can be analysed and measured can also be rearranged and manipulated for human ends, even for selfish ends. This is the tragedy of our time. So the 'throw-away' society has developed with its mountain of waste products, its pollution, spoilation of natural beauty, and its prodigal expenditure of the earth's resources, caring little for the generations to come. Having discovered how to cut the keys of the world's storehouse, the unscrupulous have raided it in order to gratify their every whim regardless of the consequences.

> 'Shall not the earth shake for this?
> Shall not all who live on it grieve?'

Thus spoke Amos.

3 New walls

But the walls could be straightened. Perhaps Amos had done as much himself. Perhaps he had tested with his plumb-line and found what he had built so crooked there was nothing for it but to knock it down and start again. A plumb-line challenges to this drastic action. So a nation can start again. This is the new preaching from the Old Testament. A people is able to turn back to God and then—this is the wonder—God himself will do the rebuilding. This is what Amos preached.

> 'On that day I will restore
> David's fallen house;
>
> I will repair its gaping walls and restore its ruins;
> I will rebuild it as it was long ago,
> that they may possess what is left of Edom
> and all the nations that were once named mine.
> This is the very word of the Lord, who will do this'
> But it is to God we must return.

25 MISSION AND PREACHING

Jonah 4.1 (NEB) '. . . I tried to escape to Tarshish.'

There is something wrong with a man's intelligence or his sense of proportion if he does not smile over the book of Jonah. This little man (or he seems little when the book that bears his name is read), commanded by God to travel east, travelled instead west. He refused to encounter the heathen away in Nineveh (and it was a tall order), but ran up against them on his doorstep at Joppa. He hid there in the hold of a ship sailing for Tarshish, but was driven up on deck by a storm. Cast overboard at his own request to appease the raging seas he discovered suicide to be no escape, for the God who produced the storm produced also a big fish to save him from drowning; only to be followed by resurrection from a watery grave and a new commission to preach God's message of judgement to the Ninevites. To his dismay, for he did not hold with missionary tours, his preaching was fantastically successful, so successful that the Ninevites repented, being delivered thereby from destruction. Whereupon Jonah fled once more, this time into high dudgeon. But he failed to escape God. In the Old Testament to make the attempt is either impossible or ridiculous, as Psalm 139 cries aloud. God made a leafy plant to provide shelter for Jonah as he sulked in a desert place overlooking the city he had hoped to see in ruins. Grateful for God's provision for his own comfort, he grew angry that God should care for the Ninevites' comfort. Then God prepared a worm to attack the leafy plant, and so it withered, causing Jonah at once to pray for death. 'I should be better dead than alive' he groaned. And the last we see of him is as a man mortally angry, sitting by the ruin of his shelter scowling at the Ninevites. Perhaps he is sitting there still, or at least, his skeleton is, unless of course the worm that ate the leafy plant ate him too . . . .

1 *Escape from mission and preaching*

There is something wrong with a man's intelligence or his

sense of proportion if he does not smile over this story, but it could be that the story is smiling at us, at the Church, the Church in the 1970s, not a winning smile, but a mocking smile, a smile like that traditionally on the face of Voltaire. The book of Jonah is a book to tease us out of our retreat from mission and preaching, depicting us as little figures in consequence, lacking much significance.

Mission has become a dirty word in some Church circles. It savours of colonialism, conversion, fanaticism, and the superior claims of one religion over another. And so we escape to dialogue with other religions, or hide away in programmes of aid or development for undeveloped countries. No doubt religious dialogue is valuable. And who will dispute that Christian aid is required of us, and that at the material level? But when dialogue, Christian aid and the service of the community are used as escape routes from mission, our name is changed to Jonah over whom we do not know whether to laugh or cry.

In the book of Jonah we have a message about mission long before colonialism existed, or even Christianity, let alone its claims to be a superior religion. Mission is proper there because God's love is *Grenzenlos* (as the Germans say), free of frontiers.

Preaching in the form of proclamation is another activity from which the Church has attempted to escape. No doubt monologue is an imperfect educational tool, but preaching is not primarily an educational activity. No doubt people respond more to what they see than to what they hear, but everything is not able to be communicated in visual form! Or why is the heart of British government a debating chamber? And why in times of stress is there a cry for the Prime Minister to address the nation? The spoken word can drive the hearers down into the death of boredom, or it can galvanise them into action. And for this reason, that the spoken word is more than a conveyor of information, it is a minister of power. So when the Church runs away from preaching, when it has no message for its generation, nothing to say, it begins to take on the features of Jonah, a pathetic escapee, hiding now in a ship's hold, now in a fish's belly, now under the shade of a leafy tree, wrapped in high dudgeon. And we do not know whether to laugh or cry.

We do not like crying, and we do in practice escape the sting of the book by classifying its material, dissecting it, searching out its origin, yes even that ridiculous story of the big fish swallowing Jonah, and of course the mention of Jonah in 2 Kings 14.25, but the book will not permit us to escape, its message pursues us as if we were Jonah in Joppa, the belly of the fish or under the shade of the leafy plant outside Nineveh, it will not suffer us to jettison mission and preaching without a conscience.

2 Rebellion

The book of Jonah begins with a flourish, which only those who read it in Hebrew can fully appreciate. 'Now the word of the Lord came unto Jonah, the son of Amittai, saying . . . .' The phrase, 'the word of the Lord' is superior to 'And God said' or 'God spoke to Jonah, the son of Amittai. . . . ' The revelation of God by his word is greater than by visions, dreams, thoughts, or any other means. The word of God is nothing less than the power of God himself. This is what came to Jonah. And the innocuous word 'came' is really tremendous. It is used in the Bible of events in nature such as the coming of rain or hail, of God dividing the light from the darkness or sending famine or earthquakes. So the commission to Jonah was a shattering experience to be followed, we would expect, by an Isaiah or Jeremiah, instead of which there appears the little man Jonah. And the content of the commission was shattering. 'Go to the great city of Nineveh.' But no prophet had hitherto been sent out of Israel to foreign parts. It is true Amos had denounced the nations, and Jeremiah was a symbol to the nations, but no one had been ordered to journey to foreign parts to denounce them, least of all, foreign parts which consisted of the mighty capital of Assyria, Nineveh.

Here then we have the story of a rebellious prophet, marking the book of Jonah as unique among the books of the Old Testament. There are books containing prophecies, but no books about the prophets themselves. The details of the lives of the great prophets can only be deduced from scattered references, but with Jonah, the opposite is true. The content of his message is meagre. We are given only one sentence. 'Yet forty days, and Nineveh shall be overthrown' (3.4 RV); but of the man himself we are given a close-up picture. Why? To show us how small a man becomes when he resists God, how impossible it is to escape God; and how that sovereignty of God over men and nature still stands whatever actions men may take to thwart it.

The message of the book of Jonah is to be sought in the absurdity of the story. Because Jonah refuses to obey the call of God that comes to him, the whole place is convulsed in storms—near ship-wreck, suicidal drowning—everything is geared to witness to the enormity of Jonah's crime in refusing God's call to mission and preaching. But his rebellion does not have the final word. Throughout the story God's sovereignty stands, and his purpose is fulfilled.

3 The content of mission and preaching

What then would God have Jonah say? What should be the content of his preaching? Jonah knows. Indeed, it is dragged out of him in one of the most moving descriptions of God in the Bible, 'a god gracious and compassionate, long suffering and ever constant, and always willing to repent of the disaster' (Jonah 4.2 NEB) God is righteous, Jonah believes this. God hates evil, Jonah believes this too. God will punish evil-doers. This also is part of Jonah's creed. What, however, he will not accept is how God's love is intertwined with God's justice. But this is the grand theme of the Old Testament. This is the new preaching.

> 'My song shall be of mercy and judgement:
> unto thee, O Lord, will I sing'
>
> (Psalm 101.1)

No one can escape mercy and judgement, because no one can escape God. He is sovereign Lord over all creatures, all people, all lands, even the regions beyond, even the worms!

And this sovereign Lord speaks after the close of the fantastic, if not ridiculous, story of Jonah which is at verse 10 of chapter 4. God comes, as it were, in front of the stage curtain to address the audience—'And should not I be sorry for the great city of Nineveh, with its hundred and twenty thousand who cannot tell their right hand from their left, and cattle without number?' (4.11) The cattle stand oddly in this context, but no more oddly than the big fish, the leafy plant and the worm in the story. God is compassionate towards all far-off creatures, whether in geographical distance, religion (or lack of religion), ignorance or in the scale of living creatures.

We ask what is the justification for mission on the part of the Church. Why should we sing our song of mercy and justice to all who are far-off? Because God has compassion on all such even in his exercise of judgement. The basis for mission and for preaching is theological and if we will not have this theology we diminish our stature. The striking feature about the book of Jonah is Jonah himself, a pathetic little figure huddled in the spaciousness of God's outreaching compassion for all men. Particularism dwarfed by universalism! Jonah could be the Church. Judaism in history followed this pattern. A crisis always arises over attitudes to mission and to preaching. If we escape from them we shall not die, but we shall look ridiculous, and then if we are proud we might as well be dead. So anyway Jonah felt. It is recorded in chapter four of the book that bears his name. In order to thwart God's commission it is better not to try to escape. . . .

26   SMALL THINGS

Zechariah 4.10 (NEB) *'Who has despised the day of small things?'*

It was 1.30 in the morning near Caterham when the car broke down. The driver's luck was out. No efforts of his succeeded in restarting the engine. He would have to journey home by other means, but there were twenty miles to go for he lived in central London. Then headlights lit up the roadway. It was a lone car, but proceeding in the wrong direction. Small chance of help there! Probably some youth racing home after revelling in the West End! But it was worth a try. So he flagged down the car and told his story. The driver was a young man. The young man listened. But without question he turned his vehicle round and drove the stranded motorist not merely to the nearest station, but the whole twenty miles back to London, depositing him at his own front door. He would take no payment. He would supply no address. Having helped the unfortunate, he drove off into the night.

A small incident! Or maybe not so small! But in an age when greed, envy and self-interest seem to be dominant in the community, surely something not to be despised.

1 *Two small men*

The text, 'Who has despised the day of small things?' derives from a depressing period of Jewish history. Wearily the inhabitants of Jerusalem were dragging themselves about the ruins of their city. They had no heart for anything. The trouble was they had returned as ex-prisoners-of-war in 538 B.C. reversing the miseries which the overthrow of their city by Nebuchadnezzar had brought about, but when they saw their city again, it was nothing like the Zion on which they had buoyed up their hopes. It lay a heap of ruins. And worse was to come. Their efforts to rebuild failed. True, a start was attempted under the leadership of two good men, Zerubbabel the Governor, and Joshua the High Priest, but they could accomplish little. The people had lost the will to work. The sense of community had broken down, and everyone drifted off to his own private interests, which, lacking co-operation, produced pathetic results. Most depressing of all, the Temple, the traditional rallying point of the people's spirits, had had its foundation laid but nothing more. Few sights are more depressing than a public building half-finished. It advertises a people's lack of enterprise.

In the midst of this depressing weariness, however, two men came to the fore. They were not great men by any standards. Granted they were called 'prophets', and two books bearing their names have found a place in the Old Testament Canon, but their words, though stirring, bore no resemblance to the utterances of Isaiah or Jeremiah. They were in fact small men with a small message in small times. Yet God spoke through them. The word of the Lord was on their lips. And true to form it did not 'return empty.' In the year 520 B.C. they got the rebuilding of the Temple started once more. Their names were Haggai and Zechariah.

But what about Zerubbabel the Governor? Remember the Hebrews had three Temples in all in their history—Solomon's, Zerubbabel's and Herod's. What about Zerubbabel in this depressing situation? Here was a man, a good man, living with failure for eighteen years till Haggai and Zechariah arose to inspire the people. What does eighteen years of frustration do to a man's soul? Is it any wonder if when Zerubbabel saw the Temple completed, he should write it off as insignificant? After all, did not those old people who could remember Solomon's glorious edifice weep when they beheld this make-shift utility model? To think that Zion had come to this! If any man needed a word from the Lord it was Zerubbabel the Governor. And he received it through Zechariah, words which have come ringing down the ages—'Who has despised the day of small things?'

2 Small actions

Not all small things are worthy of note. Much depends on the motive behind them. Jesus set out the principle when he said, 'If anyone gives so much as a cup of cold water to one of these little ones (small ones), because he is a disciple of mine, I tell you this: that man will assuredly not go unrewarded.' (St Matthew 10.42 NEB) There are records of small things set out in the gospels which did not go unrewarded. The woman who merely touched Christ's clothes and received the cure of her affliction which she had suffered twelve years. There was the small gift of five barley loaves and two small fish—a mere picnic—which a small boy allowed Jesus to use in an emergency situation, and from which five thousand men, besides women and children profited. There was Mary, who anointed Jesus with a small box of perfume she greatly prized, but the record of that feminine act has accompanied the preaching of the gospel the whole world over. There was the widow who contributed the two smallest copper coins in circulation to the Temple treasury.... And in the Old Testament there are small deeds recorded. Rahab who hid two spies as evidence that she trusted the God of Israel. David who chose five smooth stones and his shepherd's sling with which to kill a giant who mocked the living God. A widow woman in Zarephath who made a small cake for Elijah, not refusing his request though in the famine it took her last provisions. A woman in Shunem providing Elisha with a small room, a bed, a table and a candlestick, a small lodging if ever there was one, for a man to rest in as he journeyed by her house, but she did it for the God of Israel. Not all small things are worthy of note, but those that are done for God's sake do not go without reward. And the obverse of the coin should be noted. Small acts committed to defy God also do not go unrewarded. In the Old Testament there is the story of rebellious Achan and in the New Testament the story of deceitful Ananias and Sapphira. The point is—God must be taken seriously. Not even his name must be taken in vain, that is, misused. God is in the midst of life and the small things we do in respect of him whether for or against, are never without significance, because God is not without significance. Therefore, 'who has despised the day of small things?'

The question we need to ask ourselves is never, 'What is the size of my activity on behalf of God and of his people?' but, 'Have I contributed anything at all for God's sake? Have I completed my every-day tasks thoroughly instead of shoddily (which I might have done), because I believe in God? Have I been helpful and co-operative at home replacing moroseness with cheerfulness on account of the faith which I profess?' Small things? Yes, even domestic things! Nothing to compare with the accomplishments of Churchill rescuing a nation. But 'who has despised the day of small things?' They are small bricks, after all, measuring only nine inches by four-and-a-half, by three, that make up even the largest of houses. Some of us who visited Guildford Cathedral while it was in process of construction contributed the price of one brick, signing our name on it, but it was those small bricks that made up the structure which now dominates Stag Hill at Guildford.

3 Small times

We also do well to remember that there are historical periods which might be called 'small things'. Nothing of noble proportions seem to be emerging. Such is the present. The eighteenth century in England, from some angles was another such period. People had settled down. The Church had settled down. It is difficult to remember even the names of the Archbishops of that period. But even then a small thing was happening that was to have far reaching consequences. One man of small stature and donnish ways was preaching up and down the land with consequences not only for the Church but for Britain and beyond, which, no one could have guessed. This was John Wesley. 'Who has despised the day of small things?' There cannot be a harvest in the fields the whole year round. There has to be a time of seed-planting, a small time when simple work is undertaken with small seeds; but they grow with transforming results. And who would have guessed that a small tea-party in Aldersgate at the time of the Napoleonic wars when England was isolated, would have seen the commencement of the Church Missionary Society reaching out to all the world in the century which followed, and employing for some time one thousand missionaries?

'Who has despised the day of small things?' Are you another Zerubbabel, a good man but frustrated and depressed? Are you despising what you can effect in your small sphere? You are only a housewife, you say, or a business executive! Then George Herbert's hymn needs to be heard again:

> 'Teach me, my God and King,
> In all things thee to see;
> And what I do in anything
> To do it as for thee.
>
> All may of thee partake;
> Nothing can be so mean
> Which, with this tincture, "For thy sake",
> Will not grow bright and clean'
>
>   'Who has despised the day of small things?'